D0287178

ATTACK ON TITAN 34

HAJIME ISAYAMA

Episode 135:
The Battle of Heaven and Earth
3

Episode 136:
Dedicate Your Heart
49

Episode 137:
Titans
95

Episode 138:
A Long Dream
141

Final Episode:
Toward the Tree on That Hill
189

ATTACK on TITAN

Episode 135: The Battle of Heaven and Earth

...NO WONDER HE'S NOT PUTTING UP A FIGHT.
FSSSHH
HE'S ALREADY A HUSK...
SO ZEKE REALLY IS HIDING HIS OWN BODY THE WAY THE WARHAMMER TITAN DID...
WAIT... ARE YOU TELLING ME WE HAVE TO FIND A TARGET THREE FEET LONG AND FOUR INCHES ACROSS IN THIS MOUNTAIN OF BONES?!
KRAK
KRAK
THERE'S NO WAY WE CAN PULL THAT OFF!
ARMIN!!
WE NEED TO PREPARE FOR THE WORST!
I KNOW THAT !!

ONE MINUTE FROM NOW, I'LL BLOW THIS PLACE APART!!
WORK WITH THE CART TITAN AND GET AWAY!
ARMIN ...
I CAN'T IMAGINE THIS ATTACK KILLING EREN, SINCE I'M SURE HE EXPECTS IT FROM ME!!
BUT ...
BLOWING ALL THESE BONES TO PIECES MIGHT HELP US FIGURE OUT WHERE EREN AND ZEKE ARE!!
IF IT'S REALLY THAT BAD, BLOW IT ALL SKY HIGH! DON'T WORRY ABOUT US!!

...WILL NEVER BE ABLE TO CHANGE ANYTHING.
SOMEONE WHO CAN'T THROW ANYTHING AWAY...
NOTHING WILL CHANGE UNLESS I THROW THEM AWAY.
I KNOW THAT...
EREN...
I HAVE TO...
I CAN'T HOLD ONTO... MY NAÏVE HOPES...

WHA...?!
ARMIN?!
MRGH?!
SLURCH

MMMF!
NO ...!

WHAT?!

ARMIN!!

HE'S NOT MOVING...
BUT HE'S BREATHING!
LOOKS LIKE HE HIT HIS HEAD...
...DID HE COME FROM PARADIS, TOO?
HEY...!
CAN YOU HEAR ME?!
DO YOU KNOW ANNIE LEONHART?!
SHE'S MY DAUGHTER!!
...
REINER.
PLEASE, STAY ALIVE...

THE FORCES FROM PARADIS APPEAR TO HAVE...
...ENGAGED THE ATTACK TITAN.
BUT THE SPEED OF THE ENEMY'S ADVANCE HAS NOT CHANGED...
...WE CAN'T JUST SIT HERE AND WATCH.
ALL TROOPS, FIRE CANNONS AT THE ENEMY!
YES, SIR!
BUT...
THE MAJORITY OF OUR TROOPS WERE ASSIGNED TO THE AIRSHIP SQUADRON.
THE SURVIVING TROOPS CAN ONLY OPERATE THREE CANNONS AT MOST...
AND IS THAT ANY REASON TO STAND HERE WITH OUR MOUTHS AGAPE?

RIGHT NOW, ON THE BACK OF THAT MONSTROSITY...
...THERE ARE PEOPLE FIGHTING A DESPERATE BATTLE.
WHAT, EXACTLY, DO YOU THINK THEY'RE FIGHTING FOR?

REINER !! IN-COM-ING !!
BOOM
BOOOOM
AGH!!

BOOM
EA-BOOOM

WHAT ARE THESE GUYS...?
THEY'RE WAITING FOR AN OPENING AND ATTACKING IN CONCERT...
THEY DON'T ACT LIKE PURE TITANS.
IF HE'D GOTTEN SO MUCH AS A SCRATCH, HE WOULD HAVE TURNED INTO A TITAN IMMEDIATELY...
SO HE MUST BE CAPTURED, BUT COMPLETELY UNHARMED.
IS ARMIN EVEN ALIVE?!
...WHAT DO WE DO?! WE'LL RUN OUT OF THUNDER SPEARS IN NO TIME!!
—AND WAIT!

AND NOW THERE'S ALL THESE TITANS BETWEEN US AND HIM...
BUT THEY DRAGGED HIM OFF TOWARD EREN'S ASS.
SO STAY CALM.
...A FRONTAL ASSAULT ON THAT WOULDN'T BE MY FIRST CHOICE.
EVEN IF I WAS IN PEAK SHAPE...
WAIT FOR ME TO GET THEIR ATTENTION. I'LL ACT AS BAIT.
DON'T RUSH.
MIKA-SA.
THOSE ...
I'VE FIGURED OUT WHAT THEY ARE...
...THAT WON'T BE POSSIBLE, CAPTAIN...

...ARE THE NINE TITANS... FROM THROUGHOUT THE AGES.
IN OTHER WORDS, ALL THE PEOPLE WHO'VE EVER INHERITED THE POWER OF THE NINE TITANS...
I DON'T KNOW IF THEY HAVE CONTROL OF THEIR MINDS... BUT THE FOUNDING TITAN CAN PROBABLY RESURRECT THEM AGAIN AND AGAIN.
IT'S AN ARMY OF BATTLE-TESTED TITANS CREATED FOR ONE PURPOSE: TO FIGHT.
THERE'S NO WAY...
...WE CAN BEAT THAT...
CORRECT.
AND SO...
...WE CAN'T AFFORD TO STAND AROUND DELIBERATING.

AS FOR ME...
I WAS NEVER ANY FRIEND OF EREN'S.
HUH ?!
HEY!!
IS SHE ?!
PIECK ?!
AH!!
THAT LITTLE...
BOOM

ENOUGH TALK!
OUR PRIMARY TARGET HAS ALWAYS BEEN OBVIOUS!!
IT'S WHAT I'VE BEEN AIMING TO TAKE OUT FROM THE BEGINNING!
THE ATTACK TITAN'S NECK!!
FSSHT
SWOOMP
FSSHT

WAIT!!
YOU NIGHT-MARE!!
NOW GET OUT OF MY SIGHT!!
GR'K
BSSHHH
CHINK

PIECK!!
GAH!!
THWAK
FWOOSH

BA-KRAK
GALLIARD?!
OVER HERE, REINER!!
SWOOSH

PIN HIM DOWN!!
THWAK
CAPTAIN!!
UGH.
HURRY ...
GET ARMIN BACK!!

THAT'S THE ONLY WAY OUT OF THIS!!
OTHERWISE, WE'RE ALL GONNA DIE HERE LIKE DOGS!!
BOOM
GO NOW, REINER!!
PIECK...!!
JUST HOLD ON, SOME-HOW...

NOW!
...I WAS A FOOL.
ARE YOU TRYING TO STRANGLE ME...?
CAN'T STAY AWAKE...

IT'S THAT GIRL... THE FOUNDER, YMIR.
NO...
EREN...?
IF EREN IS ONLY MOVING FORWARD LIKE HE SAID HE WOULD...
...THEN THIS RESIS-TANCE IS YMIR'S WILL.
WHICH MEANS, THE FOUNDER...
...WANTS TO MAS-SACRE ALL OF HUMANI-TY, TOO...

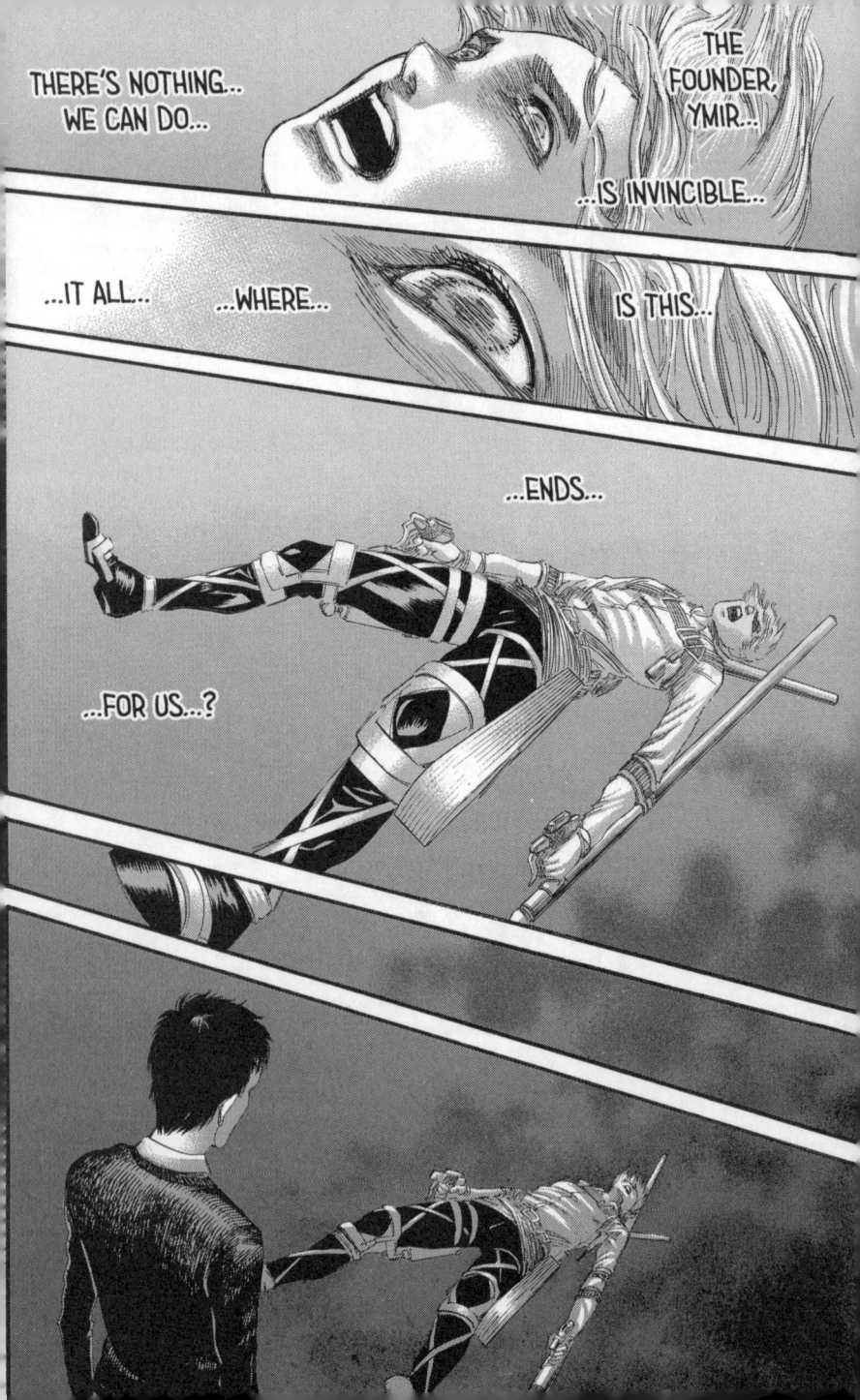
THERE'S NOTHING... WE CAN DO...
THE FOUNDER, YMIR...
...IS INVINCIBLE...
...IT ALL...
...WHERE...
IS THIS...
...ENDS...
...FOR US...?

BERTOLT?

KRUNCH
MM_MR

BOO
OOM

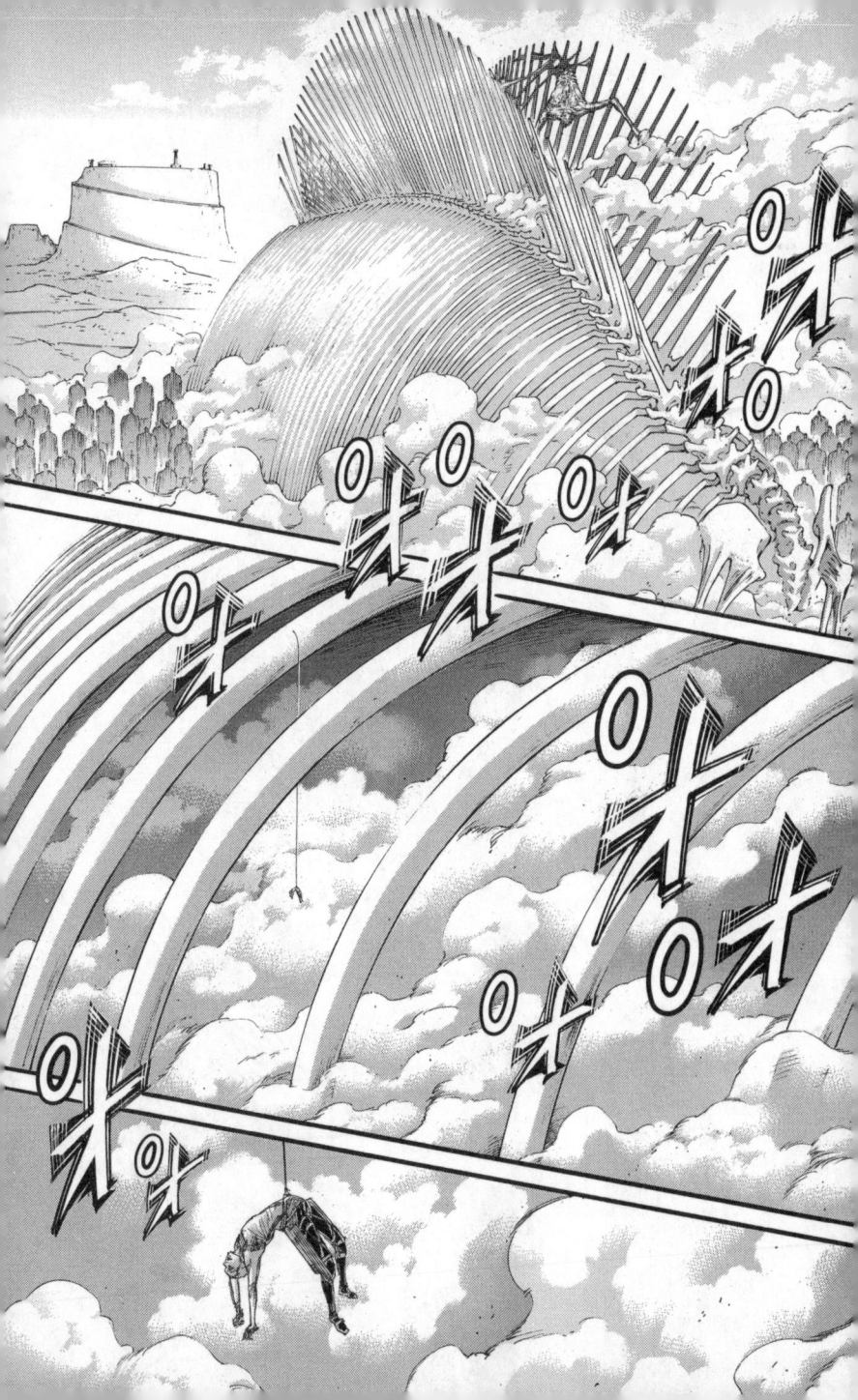

RAAH!!
SHK
WAKE UP, CONNIE!!
CAPTAIN !!
GFFH

SOR-RY...
I THINK MY MANEUVERING EQUIPMENT IS BROKEN...
MINE TOO... MY RIGHT GRIP.
IT'S SHOT.
I CAN'T PULL US UP...
KLIK KLIK

I CAN TRANS-FORM AT LEAST ONCE MORE!!
JEAN!!
LET GO!!
ZAKK
...SO YOU THINK WE CAN STILL WIN?
FOR A TITAN WITH YOUR NAME, YOU REALLY DO GET MANGLED A LOT.
THEN WHAT?! YOU GET CRUSHED BY THE RUMBLING, ARMOR AND ALL?
JEAN ...
THE SURVEY CORPS DOESN'T KNOW WHEN TO GIVE UP. THAT'S WHO WE ARE...
BUT AT LEAST...
NO...
...WE OUGHT TO DIE TRYING, RIGHT?

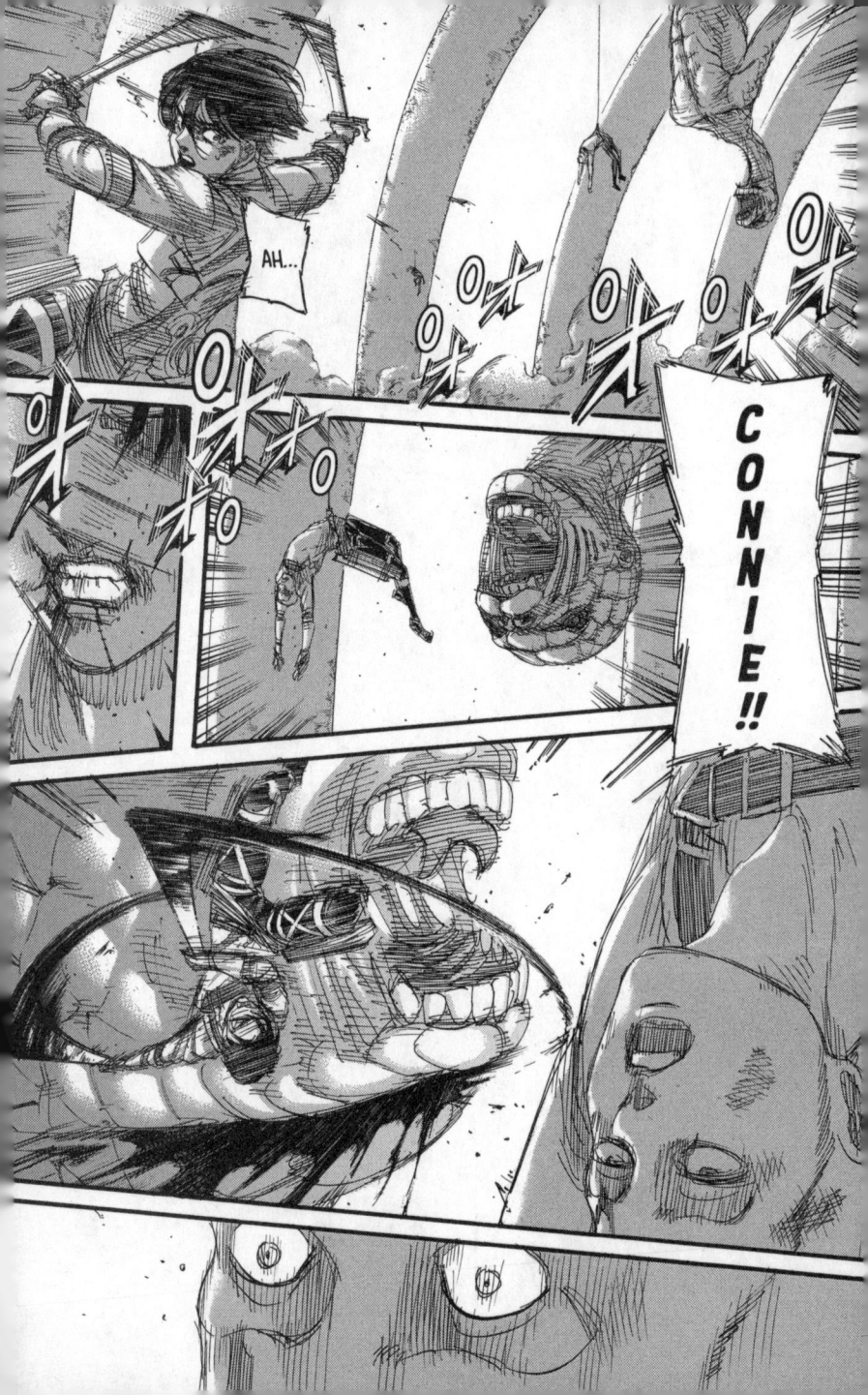
AH...
CONNIE!!

EA-
KRAK
ZSSHT
NGH!!
JERK
CAPTAIN!!
SWATCH

BRING IT ON!!
I'M STRONG !!
SO...!
COME AT ME ALL AT ONCE AND YOU'LL S–
MIKASA!! CAN YOU JUST GET OUT OF THE WAY?!
HNGH... ?!
WHA- ?!
SWATCH

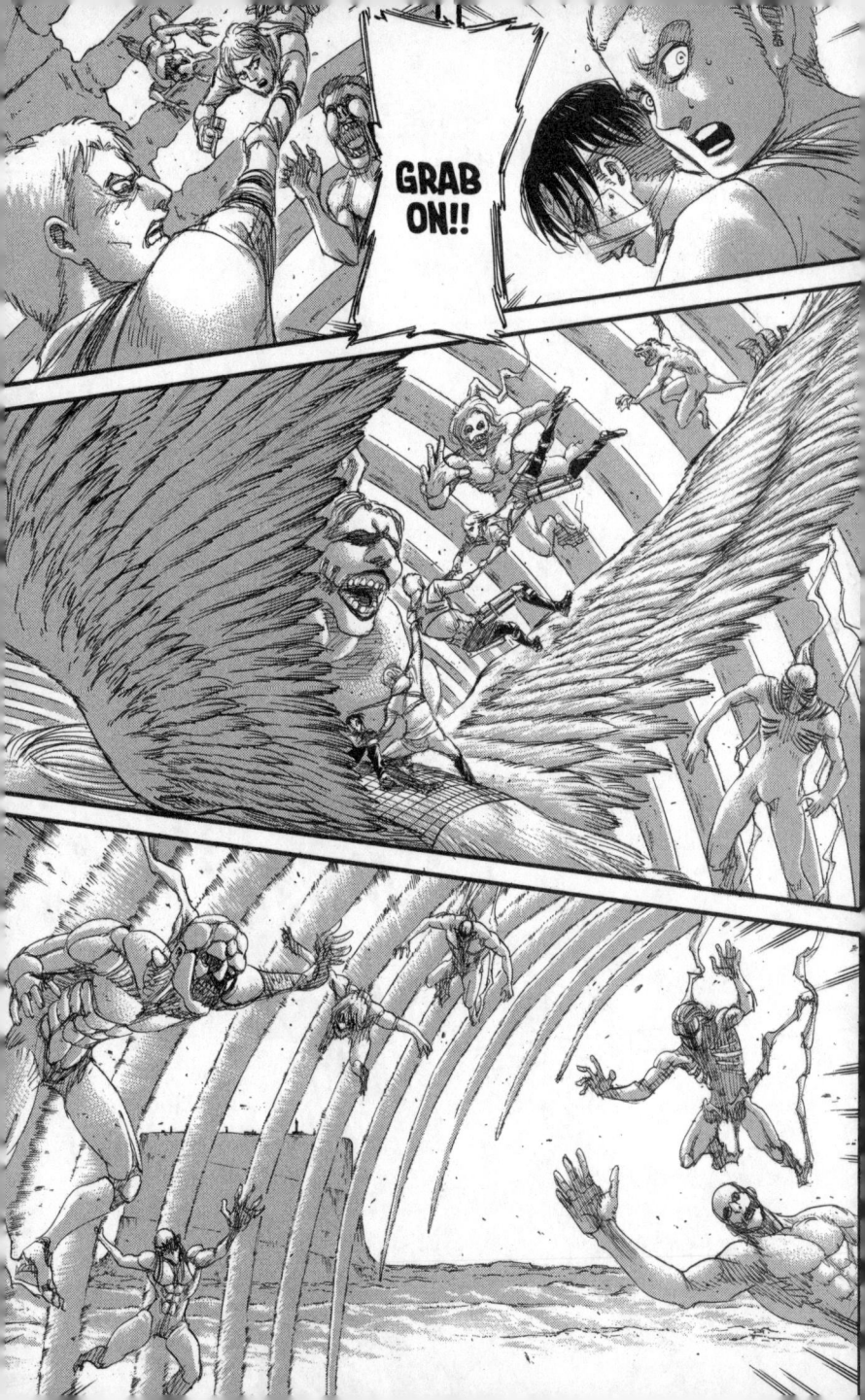
GRAB ON!!

WHOOOSH
MAN... I NEVER IMAGINED A TITAN COULD ACTUALLY FLY.

SO... I HAD TO COME.
HE REALLY DOES, THOUGH.
ANNIE!
I'M GLAD I DID.
AND...

ATTACK
on TITAN

IT'S A... BIRD...?
Episode 136: Dedicate Your Heart
AND PEOPLE ARE... RIDING ON IT...?

YOU KNOW THAT WE CAN FIGHT, TOO!
WHAT DID YOU EXPECT WHEN YOU LEFT US BEHIND LIKE THAT?!
GABI ?!
WHAT ARE YOU DOING HERE?!
...!!
WHAT ?!
THE AZUMABITO SHIP SANK.
ANNIE?!
IT COULDN'T WITHSTAND FALCO'S TRANSFORMATION...

WE WEREN'T EVEN SURE THAT HE COULD FLY...
...BUT KIYOMI KNEW ALL THAT AND LET US GO ANYWAY.
THAT'S WHY WE NEED TO STOP THE RUMBLING!
WE NEED TO REPAY HER KINDNESS!
...GABI.
FALCO.
DO YOU REMEMBER YOUR PROMISE TO ME?
OF COURSE I DO...
...MISTER BRAUN.

YOU ARE GOING TO SAVE GABI...
...FROM THE DARK, DARK FUTURE WE FACE.
I WILL...
ARMIN'S IN TROUBLE. HE'S BEEN CAPTURED BY THE TITANS.
WHAT'S HER STATUS?
HOW'S PIECK?
NO.
HOW'S ARMI...
...SO.
THE TITAN THAT TOOK ARMIN SHOULD BE BY THE TAILBONE.
I'LL GET HIM BACK.
OF COURSE.
...YOUR CHILDHOOD FRIENDS JUST LOVE GETTING KIDNAPPED, DON'T THEY...?
HELP US.
ANNIE.

BLOW IT UP?!
SHE TRIED TO BLOW THE NECK UP, BUT THE WARHAMMER TITAN WAS WAITING FOR HER.
SHE'S BY THE SKULL!
WHAT ABOUT PIECK?!
...BUT COULDN'T HIT THE TRIGGER.
SHE'S WRAPPED EXPLOSIVES AROUND THE NECK...
KOFF
WE'RE DOING... BOTH.
BOTH ...
CAPTAIN?
WE'LL SPLIT INTO TWO TEAMS... AND DO IT SIMULTAN-EOUSLY...
THE OTHER WILL GO AFTER EREN AND ATTACK THE NECK AT THE SAME TIME...
WE CAN USE THE COLOSSUS TITAN'S EXPLOSION...
ONE GROUP WILL RESCUE ARMIN...

BUT ...
NO... WE NEVER DID TO BEGIN WITH.
WE... NO LONGER HAVE THE LUXURY OF WORRYING ABOUT EREN...
WITHOUT HAVING DONE A THING...
... YEAH.
IF FALCO'S TITAN HADN'T MIRACULOUSLY BEEN ABLE TO FLY, WE WOULD'VE DIED BACK THERE!
BUT?!
BUT WHAT?!
... JEAN.
IT'S MY FAULT THAT THE CAPTAIN CAN'T EVEN FIGHT NOW!
BUT...
I DIDN'T WANT TO GIVE UP ON EREN, EITHER!
LOOK, MIKASA ...!
... DAM-MIT.
I HAD A MOUTHFUL TO SAY TO THAT IDIOT, BUT...
DO YOU REALLY THINK WE CAN AFFORD TO GO EASY ON IT?!
PLUS, WE'RE UP AGAINST THE FOUND-ING TITAN HERE!!

WE HAVE...
...TO KILL EREN.
...
MIKASA.

YOU JUST FOCUS ON SAVING ARMIN!!
MIKASA!
GRAB
...OKAY.
...TO THINK ABOUT ANYTHING ELSE...
YOU DON'T NEED...
I SHOT EREN'S HEAD OFF WITH AN ANTI-TITAN RIFLE RIGHT BEFORE HE MANAGED TO TOUCH MISTER ZEKE.
...WHAT?
WHEN EREN'S HEAD WENT FLYING...
AND IT CONNECTED TO EREN'S HEAD...
IT LOOKED LIKE A SHINING CENTIPEDE OR SOMETHING.
SOMETHING JUMPED OUT OF EREN'S SPINE...
WHEN I DID...

...WHAT? GROSS.
IF THAT'S THE FOUNDING TITAN...
NO ...
IF THAT'S THE TRUE FORM OF THE POWER OF THE TITANS...
WE MIGHT SEE IT AGAIN...
...WHEN WE DE-CAPITATE HIM.

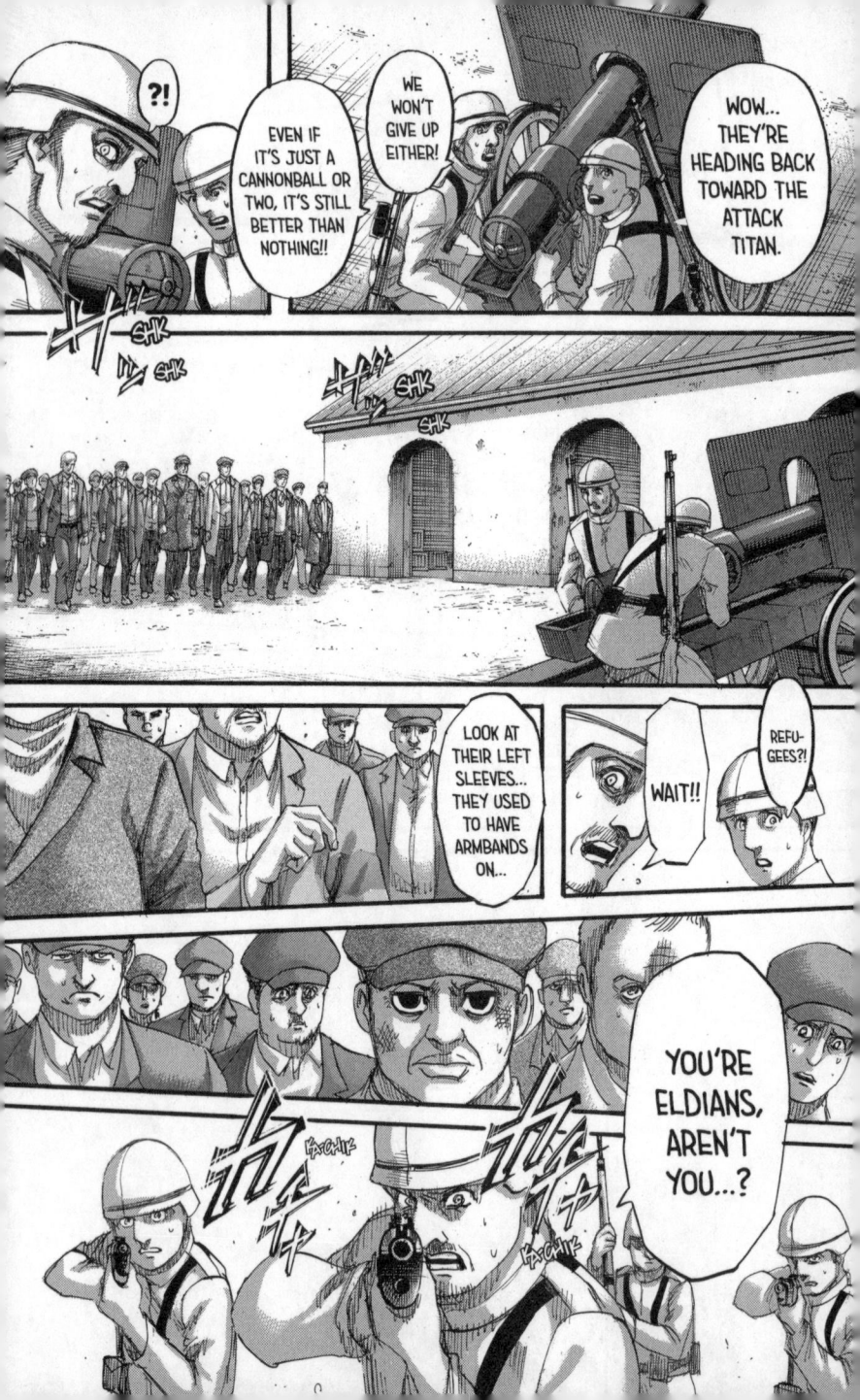
?!
EVEN IF IT'S JUST A CANNONBALL OR TWO, IT'S STILL BETTER THAN NOTHING!!
WE WON'T GIVE UP EITHER!
WOW... THEY'RE HEADING BACK TOWARD THE ATTACK TITAN.
SHK
SHK
SHK
SHK
LOOK AT THEIR LEFT SLEEVES... THEY USED TO HAVE ARMBANDS ON...
WAIT!!
REFU-GEES?!
YOU'RE ELDIANS, AREN'T YOU...?
FASCHIK
FASCHIK

HEY!!
AGH !!
SHK
SHK
HOLD ON!!
WE'RE JUST HERE TO ASK FOR HELP WITH OUR WOUNDED!!
MISTER LEONHART ...
NOW DO YOU UNDER-STAND?
WHAT ARE YOU REALLY HERE FOR?!
WE'RE IN NO SITUATION TO DO THAT!!
MARLEYAN SOLDIERS AREN'T GOING TO HELP US...
LOOKS LIKE WE OUT-NUMBER THEM.
WE HAVE MORE EXPERIENCE IN BATTLE, TOO.
WE'VE BEEN TO THE FRONT LINES, TIME AND TIME AGAIN, FOR THE SAKE OF YOU MARLEYANS, AFTER ALL.

!!
PUT DOWN YOUR GUNS, ELDIANS!!
BA-BUM
STOP !!
DAM-MIT!!
SINCE WHEN DID YOU...?
THE DRIV-ER?
WHA ?!
I SAID, PUT DOWN YOUR GUNS!!
...
SHK

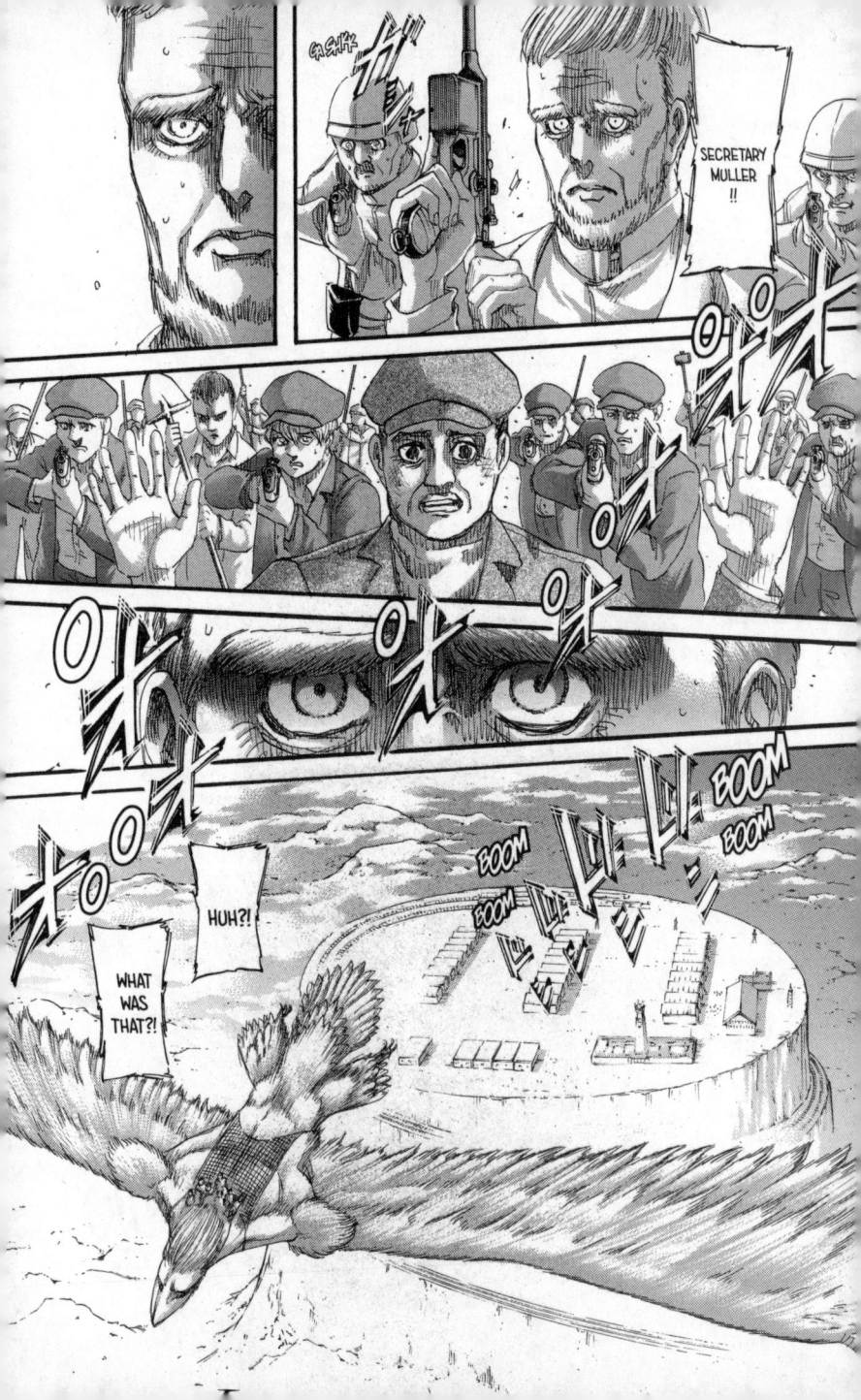
GASHA
SECRETARY MULLER !!
BOOM
BOOM
BOOM
BOOM
HUH?!
WHAT WAS THAT?!

WATCH OUT FOR PROJEC-TILES!
FALCO!!
THEY'RE STILL AT EACH OTHER'S THROATS?!
HERE THEY COME!!
NOW!!
SPEED UP!!
FWOOSH

HOLD ON!!
BOOM
BOOM
BOOM
BOOM
BOOM
WHOOSH
WHOOSH
WHOOSH

GROOOO

B
JEAN!!
REINER!!
PLEASE!!
MAKE IT OUT ALIVE!!
I'LL GET THE ATTENTION...
...OF THE WARHAMMER TITAN.
YEAH...
SAME TO YOU.

YOUR TURN...
...JEAN!!
HOLD ON...
...REINER!!

JUST UNTIL I DETONATE THE...
HISSSSSS
NGH ?!
AGH ...
MORE HELP ...?
... YEAH.
MAKES SENSE.
HISSSSSS

BSSSHHH
EEK!
THOOM
THOOM
THOOM
THOOM
TIMES LIKE THIS MAKE ME I WISH I COULD...
CHOMP
...HOP AROUND WITH THAT GEAR!

RHAK
FLASH
MMPH !!
SNAP

BOOM
DAMN IT!
I CAN'T GET CLOSE...!
WHOA!!
CHOMP
NGH!!
NO, PIECK!!
GNOOSH
BGSH
GET AWAY!!

ZSSHT
WHAT?!
JEAN...
IF YOU THINK I'M A TITAN THAT'S ONLY GOOD FOR ODD JOBS AND NOT FIGHTING...
YOU'RE DEAD WRONG.
FLASH

SNAP
ZSSH
BSSH
I CAN FIGHT UNTIL WE WIN.
...SO LONG AS THEY DON'T TAKE ME OUT...
WITH THE CART'S ENDURANCE...
FLASH

EVEN IF I HAVE TO TRY HUNDREDS OF TIMES.
SNAP
SNAP
SO...
JEAN!!
YOU DON'T NEED TO WORRY ABOUT ME! LEAVE ME AND GO TRIGGER THE B–
GWOOSH
OH.

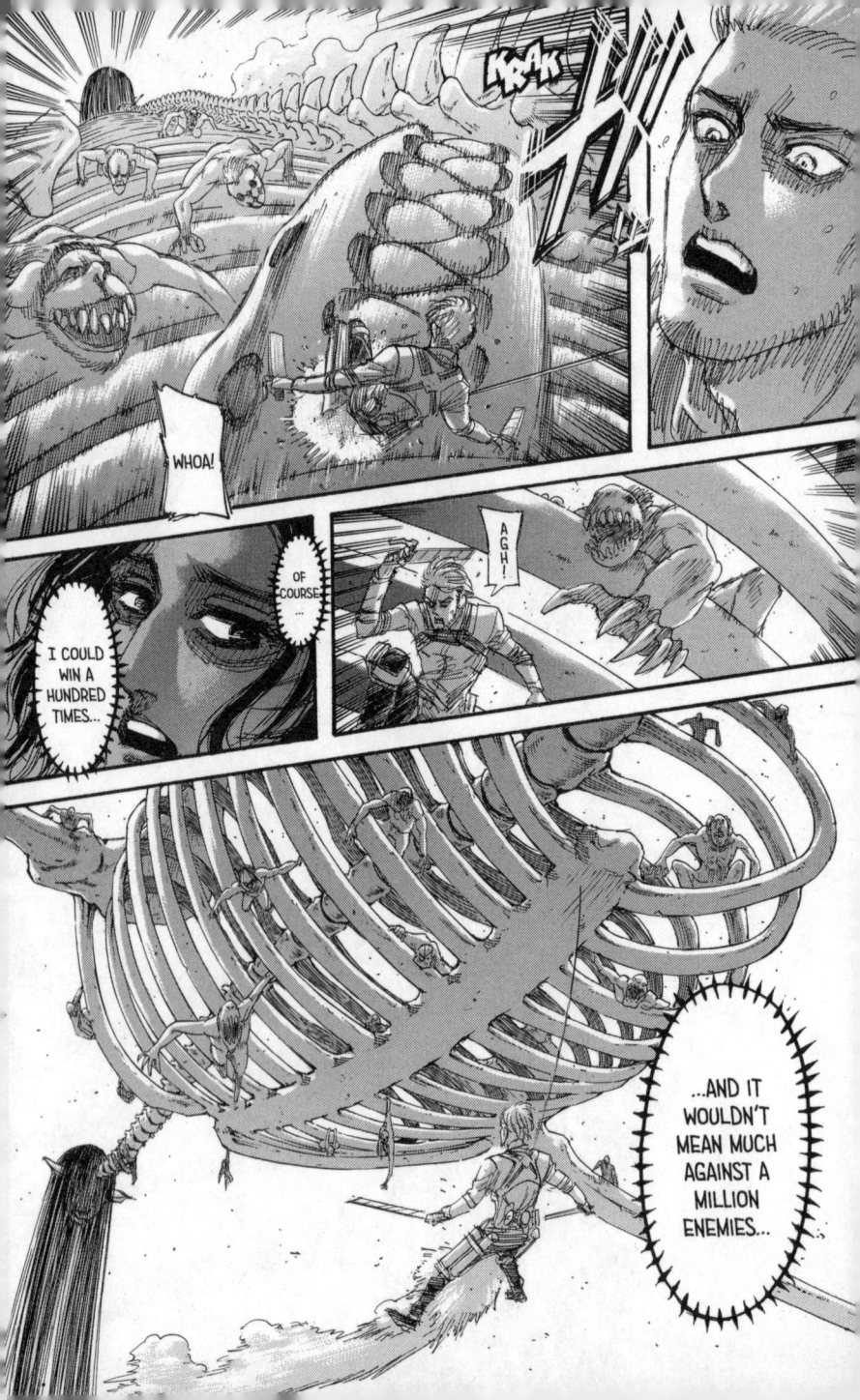
KRAK
WHOA!
AGH!
OF COURSE...
I COULD WIN A HUNDRED TIMES...
...AND IT WOULDN'T MEAN MUCH AGAINST A MILLION ENEMIES...

EVEN BERTOLT'S BEING USED AS A PUPPET...
HOW COULD THEY...
...THERE!
THAT ONE...!
THE PIG... OR WHATEVER THAT TITAN IS!!
WHICH ONE?!
THAT ONE! OVER THERE... THAT THING!
WHICH ONE?!
WHICH OF THE NINE TITANS WOULD IT BE?!
THE CART...?
THE BEAST...?
MAYBE THE JAW?
THAT DOESN'T HELP!!

I DON'T KNOW WHAT THAT IS!!
THAT?! THAT'S AN OKAPI!!
OH!! ONLY ONE IS RUNNING AWAY!!
I AM!!
MIKASA!! YOU NEED TO TAKE THIS SERIOUSLY!!
THEN WE'LL STOP IT!!
WE'LL CORNER THAT PIG OR WHATEVER IT IS WHILE IT'S ON THE TAILBONE!!
GO, FALCO!!
LET'S GET ARMIN BACK!!

FLASH
WHERE IS ZEKE...?
WHERE IS HE...?
...YOU WON'T KILL ANY OF THESE TITANS WITH THAT.
I CAN COVER YOU WITH THIS ANTI-TITAN RIFLE.
AND YET... FOR SOME REASON, HIS FINAL ORDER IS THE ONE THAT I JUST CAN'T...
NOT EVEN ONCE...
I'VE NEVER BUNGLED ONE OF HIS ORDERS...
...I'D JUST BE A BURDEN IN THIS STATE...
EVEN IF I DID FIND HIM...
DAMMIT...

COULD IT BE THAT WE FINISHED OUR MISSION...
...WAY BACK THEN?
WHEN WE GOT THOSE BRATS TO THE SEA?
DID THE PART WE HAD TO PLAY END THERE?
TELL ME...
WHEN YOU ALL DEDICATED YOUR HEARTS...
...WAS IT TO TRAMPLE ON THE HEARTS OF OTHERS?

NO.
THE DREAM YOU ALL HAD, OF A WORLD WITHOUT TITANS...
...THAT WAS AN EXHAUSTINGLY IDEALISTIC WORLD.
IF IT WAS GOING TO BE WORTH WHAT YOU DEDICATED... THE PRICE YOU ALL PAID.
IT HAD TO BE.
...ERWIN.
I...
...DIDN'T CHOOSE YOU...
AND I HAVE NO REGRETS ABOUT THAT.
GRRIP

...TO THAT KID WHO HAD THE SAME LOOK IN HIS EYES AS ALL OF YOU.
BECAUSE I ENTRUSTED THE FUTURE...

IT'S GOING TO RUN TOWARD THE HEAD.
...OH NO...
BSSHT
ANNIE !!
BSSHT
BSSHT
BSSHT
NGH !!

STOP RIGHT THERE, OKAPI!!
MGH?!
AGH!!

BOOM
BOOM
BOOM
BOOM
BOOM
AAAGH!!
OUT OF MY WAY!!
ZSSH
KLANK
ARMOR ?!
OH NO—
GRABSH

ISSK
ANNIE!!
YOU CAN'T GO OFF ON YOUR OWN LIKE THAT!!
THEY'LL KILL YOU IN NO TIME!!
THE OKAPI...
...OH NO.

IT'S HEADING FOR BERTOLT...
HEY!!
URGH.

WHY...?
WHY WON'T...
...MY BODY MOVE...?
PLEASE.
YOU HAVE TO MOVE.
EVERY-ONE'S ...
...GOING TO DIE!

REINER.
PIECK.
JEAN.
CONNIE.
MIKASA.
...ANNIE.

WAKE UP, YOU PIECE OF TRASH!!
DON'T YOU GET IT?! THEY'RE GOING TO DIE!!
ALL OF THEM!!
YOU PITIFUL COW-ARD!
YOU'RE... USE-LESS!
I HATE YOU!!
I ALWAYS HAVE!!
YOU'VE NEVER DONE ANYTHING BUT BETRAY ME!!
THE EXPEC-TATIONS, !!
THE LIFE I WAS GIVEN!!
EVERY-THING!!
YOU KEEP LETTING EVERYONE DOWN!!
ALL OF IT!!
THE RESPONSI-BILITIES!!

I SAID MOVE!!
MOVE!!
HOW DARE YOU DIE LIKE THIS?!
HOW DARE YOU?!

... SAND.
THINK.
IF I REALLY WAS DEAD, HOW WOULD I BE ABLE TO THINK WITH NO OXYGEN COMING TO MY BRAIN?
THIS ...
...ISN'T A DREAM.
IT'S NOT A VI-SION.
IT'S NOT EVEN THE AFTERLIFE...
IT'S THE PATHS.
THIS IS REAL!!

...I'M SUPPOSED TO BE IN A TITAN'S MOUTH RIGHT NOW.
SO WHY DO I KNOW WHAT EVERYONE'S DOING...?
...BECAUSE ALL ELDIANS ARE CONNECTED VIA THESE PATHS?
BUT THAT MEANS ...
THERE MIGHT BE... SOMETHING I CAN DO HERE.
YEAH.
THINK.
THINK!!

...
WH...

HELLO.
MIS-TER ZEKE.
EREN'S FRIEND.
HELLO ...
SO, YMIR ATE YOU TOO...?

ATTACK on TITAN

LONG, LONG AGO...
...THERE WAS A TIME WHEN NOTHING BUT MERE MATTER EXISTED IN THIS WORLD.
IN THE TEEMING OOZE, FORMS OF A CERTAIN **SOMETHING** APPEARED, DISAPPEARED, AND APPEARED AGAIN...
...AND ONE OF THEM EVENTUALLY SURVIVED.
WE NOW KNOW IT AS "LIFE."

Episode 137: Titans

THIS SAND.
THESE PEBBLES.
THE WA-TER.
THEY DON'T SEEK TO MULTIPLY.
BUT LIFE NEVER STOPS IN ITS FRANTIC QUEST TO DO SO.
AND DEATH...
...THAT IS, EXTINCTION OF THE SPECIES, RUNS COUNTER TO THE GOAL OF MULTIPLYING.
THAT IS WHY WE FACE THE PUNISHMENT KNOWN AS FEAR.
...AND WHY THAT CHILD SO DESPERATELY SOUGHT TO AVOID SUCH PAIN.
GREATER POWER.
GREATER SIZE.
SHE GAVE BIRTH TO AN UNDYING BODY.
AND THEN SHE ESCAPED TO A WORLD THAT WAS FREE...
...EVEN OF DEATH.

...WHAT EXACTLY... IS YMIR'S GOAL?
BUT IF THAT'S TRUE...
...IS THAT WORLD FREE OF DEATH.
AND THIS...
THAT GIRL WAS YMIR, THE FOUNDER...
WHY WAS THAT...?
IN SPITE OF ALL THE STRENGTH SHE HAD, SHE COULD NEVER DEFY KING FRITZ.
...TRYING TO UNDERSTAND HER.
...I MYSELF SPENT AN ASTOUNDING AMOUNT OF TIME HERE...
...SHE REMAINED HERE, OBEYING HIM. WHAT WAS THE REASON?
FOR TWO THOUSAND YEARS...
SHE DID STILL FEEL ATTACHED TO THE WORLD SHE LEFT BEHIND...
YES...

EREN WAS ABLE TO UNDERSTAND THAT...
...WHEN I COULDN'T.
AND THAT IS WHY YMIR...
...CHOSE HIM.
...YOU HAVE TO TELL ME!
ISN'T THERE... SOME WAY OF GETTING BACK TO THE OUTSIDE WORLD FROM HERE?!
WHO KNOWS ...
I THINK IT'S IMPOSSIBLE NOW...
I HAVEN'T GIVEN UP YET.
...
WHY NOT...?

IS THE CONTINUED EXISTENCE OF YOUR SPECIES REALLY THAT IMPORTANT TO YOU?
YOU STILL SEEK TO MULTIPLY?
WELL ...
A FEAR BORN OF LIFE-SUSTAINING FUNCTIONS THAT ARE COMPLETELY WITHOUT MEANING AND...
...ARE THE PITIFUL DEATH THROES OF LIFE FORMS CONTROLLED BY FEAR.
ONE MIGHT SAY WHAT WE'RE WITNESS-ING...
WHAT WE'RE DOING IS FIGHTING FEAR!!
BECAUSE WE CAN STILL SAVE SO MANY PEOPLE FROM TERROR...!!
MY FRIENDS... THEY'RE FIGHTING RIGHT NOW!!
YOU KNOW THAT TO LIVE...
...MEANS TO ONE DAY DIE, DON'T YOU?
AND WOULD IT BE SO WRONG TO LOSE THAT FIGHT?

WHO KNOWS...
PERHAPS ONE'S FINAL MOMENTS...
...BRING SOME KIND OF RELIEF.
THE END OF A LIFETIME BEING MANIPULATED...
...ALL IN THE NAME OF GROWTH...
...WITHOUT EVER KNOWING IF IT MEANS ANYTHING AT ALL.

THAT SOUNDS LIKE FREEDOM TO ME...

WE WANTED TO SEE WHICH OF US WOULD GET THERE FIRST.
WE WERE RUNNING TO THE TREE ON THE HILL.
THE SUN WAS STARTING TO SET.
AND I, OF COURSE, WAS DEAD LAST...
MIKASA RAN TOO, BUT STAYED BEHIND HIM ON PURPOSE...
EREN SHOUTED THAT IT WAS A RACE AND TOOK OFF OUT OF NOWHERE...
...FOR SOME REASON, A THOUGHT CAME TO ME.
AND ...
LEAVES FLUTTERED EVERY-WHERE.
IT FELT GOOD JUST TO RUN.
BUT... THE BREEZE WAS NICE AND WARM THAT DAY.

MAYBE ...
...THE REASON I WAS BORN...
...WAS SO THAT THE THREE OF US COULD RUN THIS RACE, ON THIS DAY.

I THOUGHT THE SAME THING LATER, READING A BOOK ON A RAINY DAY.
AND WHEN I GAVE A SQUIRREL SOME NUTS, AND IT ATE THEM.
AND WHEN WE WALKED AROUND THE MARKET.
...IT CAME TO ME AGAIN.

THAT...
...THESE TRIVIAL MOMENTS...
...MIGHT ACTUALLY BE PRECIOUS...
THAT...
THIS...?
IT WAS BURIED IN THE SAND...
...
WHY IS THAT...
WHO KNOWS...
BUT... TO MY EYES...
...EVEN IF THERE'S NO NEED FOR SOMETHING LIKE THIS IN ORDER TO MULTIPLY...
...IT'S STILL INCREDIBLY PRECIOUS.

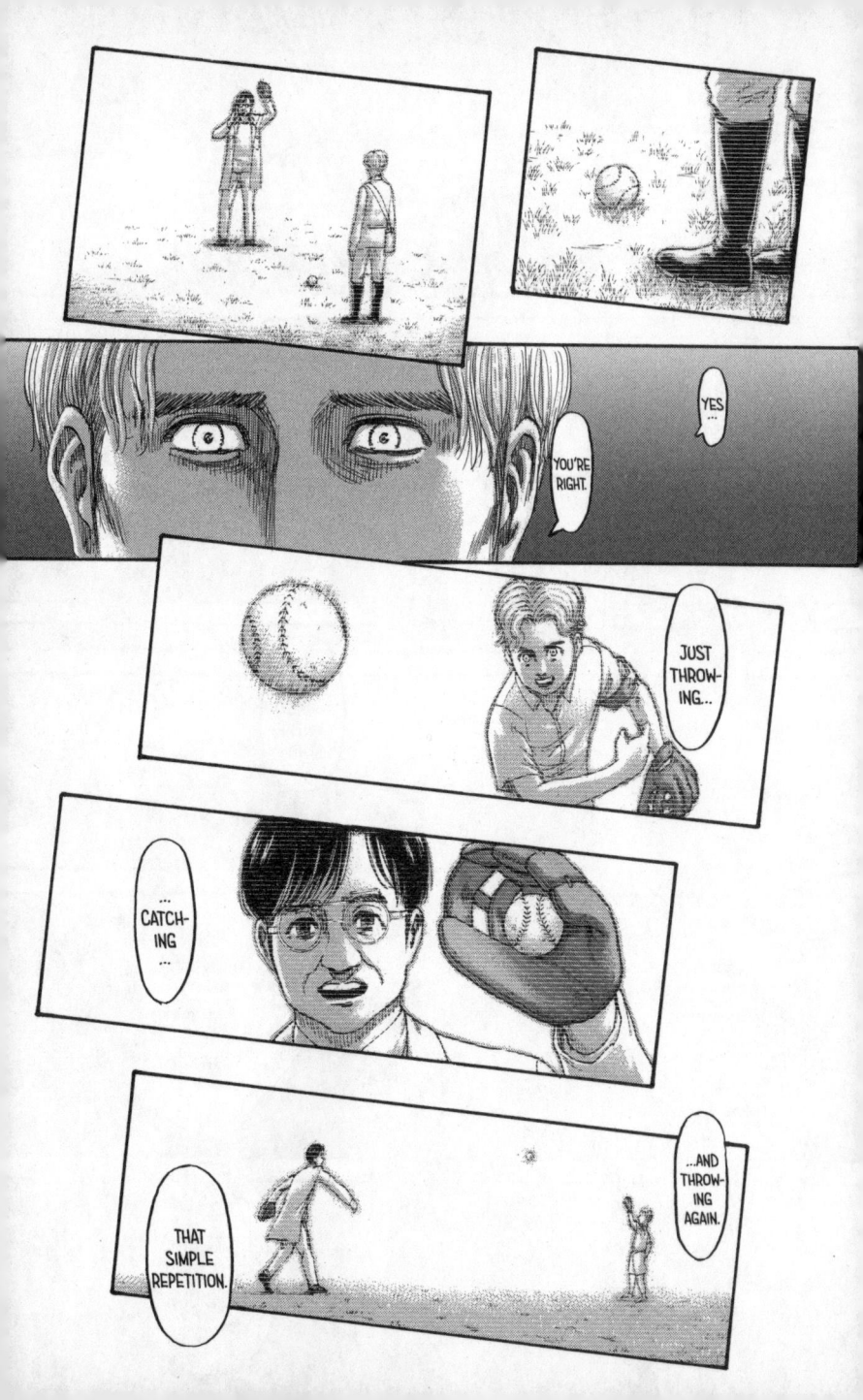
YES...
YOU'RE RIGHT.
JUST THROW-ING...
...CATCH-ING...
...AND THROW-ING AGAIN.
THAT SIMPLE REPETITION.

IT DOESN'T MEAN A THING...
BUT...
YOU'RE RIGHT...
I...
...WOULD HAVE BEEN HAPPY PLAYING CATCH FOREVER.

PIECK!!
UGH
KHOOSH

WE NEED TO RETREAT BACK TO WHERE REINER–
YOU'RE DONE!!
...I CAN KEEP FIGHTING ONCE MY ARM'S HEALED...
REINER!!

NGH ...!!
JEAN!!
PIECK!!
MGH!!

BOOM
UGH!!
ANNIE!!

BOOM
WHAT THE ?!

BERTOLT...

WHAT?!
...?!
PORCO!!
SNAP
MARCEL!!
GALLIARD!!
WHA ?!
BOOM

YMIR...?!
DID HE JUST SAVE US?!
BER-TOLT ?!
...
...I DON'T KNOW...
BUT...
I WON'T WASTE THIS CHANCE!!
SHINGGG
BAM

BOOM
I HIT IT !!
KGGGT
WHOOSH
GIVE... AR-MIN...
SCRRRK
SSHK
BACK!!

ARMIN!!
BLAMM
WHA?!
ZSSK

HRAAGH!!
AGH!!
WHOOSH
ANNIE !!
TIC
WHOOOSH

THUD
BOOM
BOOM
BOOM
BOOM
BOOM
BOOM
BOOM
BOOM
ANNIE ...
ARMIN...
KUOFF KUOFF
SORRY...
BUT ...
I'M OKAY NOW.
EVERYONE...
BOOM
BOOM
BOOM
BOOM
BOOM
BOOM
BOOM
ANNIE!!
BEHIND YOU!!
!!

WHAT'S GOING ON?!
THE TITANS ARE HELPING US?!
SEEMS THAT WAY.
HEEY !!
HEEEEY!
OVER HEE-ERE!
WHAT ...?
NO WAY ...

...ZEKE.
I CAN'T SAY I MISSED YOU!!
YOU MISSED ME, DIDN'T YOU, LEVI?!
TH-THMP
ZEKE ?!
WHAT THE HELL'S GOING ON?!
IT'S THANKS TO MISTER ZEKE...
...IN THE WORLD OF THE PATHS, WHERE NEITHER LIFE NOR DEATH HAS MEANING.
HE WOKE UP EVERYONE WHO WAS ASLEEP...

EVERY ELDIAN IS CONNECTED TO ONE ANOTHER BY THE PATHS.
I THINK...
...IT'S BECAUSE THE FOUNDER, YMIR, WANTED TO BE CONNECTED.
BECAUSE SHE WANTS SOMETHING FROM US...
BER-TOLT...
MISTER KSAVER.

WE NEVER ACHIEVED OUR DREAM...
AND I STILL DON'T THINK THE EUTHANIZATION PLAN WAS A MISTAKE...
BUT ...
IF IT MEANT GETTING TO PLAY CATCH WITH YOU AGAIN, I GUESS...
...I WOULDN'T MIND LIVING AGAIN, AFTER ALL.
SO... I GUESS I SHOULD THANK YOU.
FA-THER.
I TOOK EVERYTHING FROM YOU.
YOUR LIFE...
...EVEN YOUR PRECIOUS MEMORIES.
YOUR POWER ...
THAT'S WHY I KNOW.
WE CAN'T JUST STAY HERE.

PLEASE HELP ME.
...WHAT A BEAUTIFUL DAY IT IS.
...I WISH I HAD SEEN IT EARLIER.
I SUP-POSE ...
AFTER ALL THE KILLING I'VE DONE...
...THAT'S TOO MUCH TO ASK.

SSSHK

THE RUMBLING...
IT STOPPED ...?

JEAN!!
...
GO!!

SNATCH
GOOD-BYE...
...YOU SUICIDAL BLOCK-HEAA AAAAAAAADD
KLIK

B
M

AAAGH!

THERE IT IS!!
IT'S GOING AFTER EREN'S HEAD!
IT'S DOING IT AGAIN...?!
BOOM

!!
REINER!!
BOOM
JEAN!
PIECK !!
WE NEED TO GET AWAY, QUICK!!
ARMIN'S GONNA BLOW THOSE BONES TO PIECES!!

AND ANY-WAY...
THE ARMORED TITAN SHOULD PROTECT HIM FROM THE EXPLOSION.
...WAIT! REINER'S STILL—!!
REINER KNOWS EXACTLY WHAT IT WILL MEAN...
...IF WE LET THIS OPPORTUNITY SLIP AWAY.

...THANK YOU.
WITHOUT ALL OF YOUR HELP...
...WE WOULDN'T HAVE BEEN ABLE TO STOP THE RUMBLING.

GOOD-BYE...
...EREN.

ATTACK on TITAN

Episode 138:
A Long Dream

URGH...
...WHAT HAP-PENED ...?!
ALL THOSE BONES EXPLOD-ED!!
SIS!
ARE YOU OKAY ?!
AGH ...

LOOK!
THE BONES ARE GONE...
THE RUMBLING HAS STOPPED, TOO...
IS EREN... DEAD...?
AGH!!
THROB
...I WAS A KID...
EVER SINCE...
AN UNDOUBTING SLAVE WHO ALWAYS FOLLOWED ORDERS WITHOUT QUESTION.
THEY OFTEN SUFFER FROM SUDDEN HEADACHES.
ONCE AN ACKERMAN AWAKENS,

THROB
...IT CAN'T BE...
I'VE ALWAYS HATED YOU.
MIKASA.
THROB
THAT ...
...CAN'T BE OUR LAST...

WE...
BUT ...
...IT'S NOT LIKE I DON'T HAVE REGRETS.
WE STOPPED THE RUMBLING.
...DID THE RIGHT THING, DIDN'T WE?

YOUR FATHER.
MISTER LEONHART LED US ALL HERE.
ALL THE WAY FROM THE INTERN-MENT ZONE...
...HOW'D YOU GET HERE?
GO AND SEE HIM.
YES... I SAW.
REINER'S STILL FIGHTING!!
AUNT KARINA!
...!!
ARMIN.
REINER... WHERE ARE THEY?!
THAT SHINING CENTIPEDE ...

REINER!!
HE'S OKAY...
HEY... LOOK!!
OVER THERE!!
IT GOT HIT BY THAT EXPLOSION... AND SURVIVED?!
WHAT THE HELL IS THAT THING...?!
RUMBLE
RUMBLE
RUMBLE
RUMBLE
THOOM
WHO KNOWS...
ALL I CAN SAY FOR SURE IS THAT WE CAN'T LET IT LIVE.
RUMBLE
RUMBLE
RUMBLE
RUMBLE

FLASH
WELL... FIGURES...
I DIDN'T THINK THAT'D BE ENOUGH TO KILL YOU...
YEAH...
BUT.
WHAT DO WE DO NOW?

...EREN.
THOOM

THERE'S NO TELLING WHAT COULD HAPPEN!!
YOU CAN'T LET THAT SHINING THING COME IN CONTACT WITH EREN!
...OH NO.
THAT THING...
...EVEN START THE RUMBLING AGAIN...
IT MIGHT...
WE NEED TO GO...
...HOW DO WE KILL SOMETHING THAT SURVIVED THAT EXPLOSION JUST NOW?
WE'VE GOTTA KILL THAT SHINING THING!!
THIS NIGHTMARE WON'T END UNTIL WE TAKE HIM DOWN...
YOU UNDERSTAND BY NOW, RIGHT...?
...FOR EREN.
...AND COLT'S, TOO.
I'M COMPLETING MY MISSION...
I STILL HAVE ONE FINAL JOB.
FATHER.

...DID IT TURN OUT LIKE THIS?
...WHY?
THROB
THOM
HOW...
THROB
THOM
NGH?!
BOOM
BOOM
BOOM
...WHAT ?!
BSSSSH

THANK YOU.
GONE
NO...IT'S AN OLD INJURY.
IS YOUR LEG HURT?!
I NEED HELP DEPLOYING CANNONS!
THE TITANS ARE STILL CLOSING IN!
BRING THE INJURED HERE!
CAN YOU STAND ?
...WE'D STILL BE AT EACH OTHER'S THROATS.
IF YOU HADN'T FIRED ALL THOSE ROUNDS INTO THE AIR, I IMAGINE...
DAD.
YES ...
BUT LET'S WORK TOGETHER TO OVERCOME THIS...
I'VE MADE MY FAIR SHARE OF MISTAKES...
ANN... IE...?

WHAT IS...
...THAT SMOKE ?!
THE SMOKE'S COMING FROM THAT SHINING THING.
KOFF
KOFF
DID IT DIE?
NO ...
THAT'S NOT THE SMELL OF A DEAD TITAN.

ISN'T THIS ...
KOFF
...THE SAME THING ...
...THEY DID IN RAGAKO ...?
...MI-KA-SA!!
PIECK !
GET ON FALCO!
GET AWAY FROM HERE!!
HUH ...?!
WHAT ...
...ARE YOU SAY-ING?
ACKERMANS AND ANYONE WITH THE POWER OF THE TITANS WON'T BE AFFECTED.
YOU SHOULD KNOW WHAT WE NEED TO DO BETTER THAN ANYONE HERE.
...
NO.
HURRY AND GO!!
THIS IS TOO MUCH FOR ME TO—

HELP
WE'LL HAVE TO TRUST THEM TO FINISH THIS.
...GUESS SO.
...IS HOW IT ENDS FOR US.
SO THIS...
THE NIGHT WE HAD TO BURN THOSE BODIES?
...DO YOU REMEMBER, JEAN?
THAT'S WHAT IT MEANS TO DIE AS A MEMBER OF THE SURVEY CORPS.
THAT WE ENDED UP STUCK WITH THE JOB OF SAVING HUMANITY...
...YOU KNOW THIS IS ALL YOUR FAULT, RIGHT?
...YEAH.

KRAK
KRAK
KRAK
KRAK
KRAK
KRAK
KRAK
KRAK
NO WAY...
HOW CAN THIS REALLY BE HAPPENING...?

ARE YOU OKAY ?!
HEY!!
WHAT ...
...IN THE WORLD HAP-PENED ?!
NGH ...?!
D... DAD?!
...SIR!!

AAAH...!
BOOM
BOOM
BOOM
BOOM
BOOM
BOOM
BOOM
BOOM
BOOM
BOOM
BOOM
BOOM
BOOM

...ARE YOU OUT OF YOUR MIND?!
...YOU SUMMONED YOUR TROOPS.
SO...
THERE'S NO WAY YOU'RE GETTING PAST ME!!
BOOM
BOOM
BOOM
BOOM
BOOM
BOOM
BOOM
BOOM
BOOM
BOOM
BOOM
BOOM

THOOM
YOU REALLY ...
...LOVE MAKING LIFE HELL, DON'T YOU...
... EREN?!
THOOM
FINE, THEN...
I'LL KEEP DOING THIS WITH YOU UNTIL THE BITTER END!!
THOOM

AAAGH!
BOOM
BOOM
BOOM
BOOM
BOOM
BOOM
BOOM
CONNIE?
JEAN...?
GABI?
MOM?!
HOW?!
IT CAN'T BE...
WHOOSH!

CHOMP
PIECK...
ANNIE...
AAAAAHHH!
G
R
R
S
H
T
...FOR OUR EFFORTS TO FINALLY PAY OFF?
WHAT MUST WE DO...

THROB
WE'RE THE ONLY ONES LEFT WHO CAN KILL EREN!!
STAY WITH ME HERE!
MIKASA?!
AARGH!!
...TAKE...
...ANY MORE OF THIS.
I CAN'T...
THROB
THROB

...I WANT TO GO HOME...
I JUST...
...WANT TO GO BACK...
...HOME...

MI-KA-SA.
WAKE UP.

YOU'LL CATCH A COLD.

HUH?
...I...

...EREN?

WHEN DID I FALL ASLEEP...?

LET'S JUST TAKE IT EASY FOR THE REST OF TODAY.

I MANAGED TO CATCH A BIG FISH, AFTER ALL...

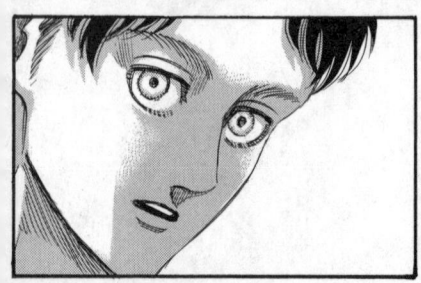

YOU MUST'VE BEEN EXHAUSTED...
I FEEL LIKE...
...I JUST HAD A LONG DREAM.

MIKASA...
WHY... ARE YOU CRYING?

...HUH?

I...
...SUDDENLY WASN'T SURE I BELONGED HERE...

I WONDER WHY...

YOU KNOW...
...THERE'S NOTHING WE CAN DO ABOUT IT NOW...
HUH?
THE TWO OF US...
...ABANDONED EVERYTHING.
SINCE THE DAY WE ESCAPED OUT HERE...
SINCE THE WAR WITH MARLEY ENDED... IT'S BEEN TWO MONTHS.
THE INVASION OF PARADIS WILL BEGIN SOON...

RUNNING AWAY IS THE ONLY WAY FOR ANYONE TO SURVIVE...
I BET ARMIN...
...IS LOOKING ALL OVER FOR US RIGHT NOW.
I...
...COULDN'T SEND HISTORIA TO HELL...
...AND CONTINUE THAT ENDLESS SLAUGHTER.
AND I COULDN'T DESTROY ALL OF HUMANITY OUTSIDE THE WALLS...
SO WHY NOT CHOOSE...
...TO LIVE THE FOUR YEARS I HAVE LEFT IN PEACE AND QUIET...
...WHERE NOBODY ELSE IS AROUND...
JUST THE TWO OF US?
MIKASA. WASN'T IT...
...YOU...
...WHO ASKED ME THAT?

...YES.
I'M SOR-RY.
I KNOW I PROMISED I WOULDN'T BRING THIS UP...
THROW THIS SCARF OUT ONCE I'M DEAD...
...WILL YOU MAKE ME ONE MORE PROMISE?

YOU HAVE A LONG LIFE AHEAD OF YOU...
SO FORGET ABOUT ME.
BE FREE...
PLEASE...
MIKASA.
FORGET ABOUT ME.

I'M SORRY.

I CAN'T DO THAT.

EREN...
...IS INSIDE THE MOUTH.
I'LL DO IT.
EVERYONE COVER ME.

UNDER-STOOD...
...MIKASA.

SEE YOU LATER...
...EREN.

ATTACK on TITAN

HEY, I GET IT... YOU DID IT FOR THE SAKE OF THE FUTURE YOU SAW USING THE ATTACK TITAN'S POWER.
BUT DID YOU REALLY HAVE TO BEAT ME TO A PULP...?
WHY?
WAS KNEEING ME THAT IMPOR-TANT?

I WAS SO DESPERATE TO PUSH YOU ALL AWAY...
EVEN I FOUND MYSELF WONDERING WHAT I WAS DOING... I JUST LET THE MOMENT TAKE OVER... REALLY.
... SORRY.

Final Episode: Toward the Tree on That Hill
YOU SHOULD BE SAYING THAT TO MIKASA, NOT ME.
ALL THAT NONSENSE YOU SPEWED HURT HER...
YEAH...
YOU'RE RIGHT.

IT WAS ALL...
...TO PUSH US AWAY FROM YOU...
...AND MAKE US INTO HEROES WHO SAVED HUMANITY FROM EXTINCTION BY HUNTING YOU DOWN?
...
THAT'S RIGHT.
HOW COULD YOU NOT BE SEEN AS SAVIORS BY EVERY SURVIVING HUMAN BEING?
YOU TURNED YOUR BACKS ON PARADIS IN SPITE OF BEING "ISLAND DEVILS" TO STAND ON THE SIDE OF HUMANITY TO THE END.
YOU'D BECOME THE MOST RESPECTED PEOPLE IN THIS WORLD.

HUH ?

THEY WON'T BE ABLE TO RETALIATE IMMEDI-ATELY.
WE'RE SUPPOSED TO PROTECT PARADIS FROM REPRISAL FROM HUMANITY OUTSIDE THE WALLS?
...SO YOU WANT US TO BE LIKE THE TYBUR FAMILY AFTER THE GREAT TITAN WAR?

THEY'LL LOSE THE CAPACITY TO WAGE WAR.
THE RUMBLING WILL KILL EIGHTY PERCENT OF HUMANITY.

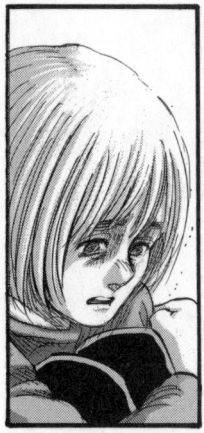

DID YOU ...
... REALLY NEED TO GO THIS FAR?
WAS THIS..
...ALL FOR OUR SAKE?
WHERE ARE YOU...?
WHERE WE WANTED TO GO.
LET'S TALK AS WE WALK.
...ABOUT OUR FOUNDER, YMIR.

SO THIS...
...IS BURNING WATER.
IT REALLY IS FLOWING LIKE A RIVER...

...

...WHERE DID I LEAVE OFF?
...HM?
YOU SAID THAT THE POWER OF THE TITANS CONTINUES TO EXIST BECAUSE YMIR HAS BEEN OBEYING KING FRITZ FOR 2,000 YEARS...

...
...SHE CONTINUED TO OBEY HIM.
BUT EVEN WHEN SHE ATTAINED GOD-LIKE POWERS...
HE'D BURNED HER HOMETOWN, KILLED HER PARENTS... AND PULLED OUT HER TONGUE.
RIGHT...

I COULDN'T BELIEVE IT, BUT...
...I FELT SOME-THING.
WHEN WE TOUCHED IN THE PATHS...

...COULD HAVE CAUSED HER TO DO THAT...?
WHAT...

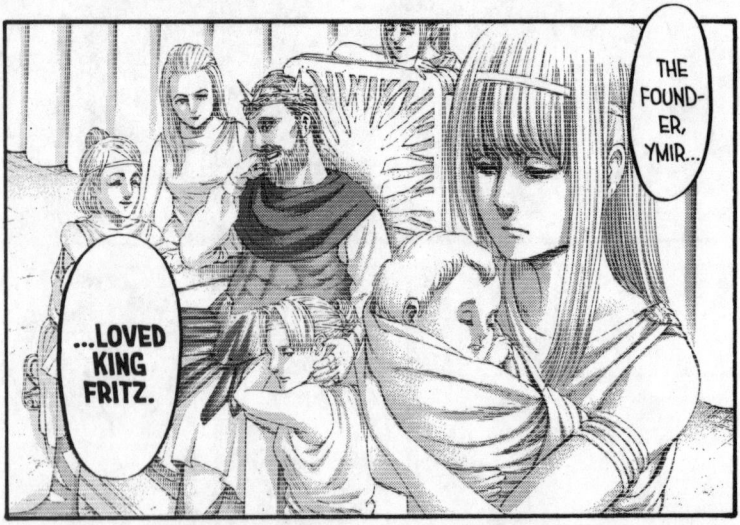
...LOVED KING FRITZ.
THE FOUND-ER, YMIR...

THAT'S WHAT BOUND HER FOR OVER TWO THOUSAND YEARS.
...WHAT?
...

THEN, THAT SOMEONE APPEARED.

IT WAS MIKASA.

HUH?
DID YOU JUST SAY MIKASA?
...I DID.
SO YOU WEREN'T LISTENING AFTER ALL...
I WAS!
WHY MIKASA ...?
WELL ...
ONLY YMIR KNOWS THAT ONE...
AS FOR ME...
...EVEN I STILL DON'T KNOW...
..WHAT MIKASA WILL DO.

THE ONLY THING I KNOW FOR SURE...
...IS THE RESULT OF MIKASA'S CHOICE.
ALL OF IT... HAS BEEN TO ARRIVE AT THAT RESULT.
THAT'S WHY...
...I MOVED FOR-WARD.
KILLING EIGHTY PERCENT OF HUMANITY.
FORCING YOU TO FIGHT EACH OTHER ON PARADIS.
GETTING EVEN MY PRECIOUS FRIENDS...
...WRAPPED UP IN THIS BATTLE, WITHOUT EVEN KNOWING IF YOU'D SURVIVE IT.
THAT ...
...WAS THE FUTURE YOU SAW AT THE MEDAL CEREMONY ...
YOU'VE BEEN ALL ALONE SINCE THEN...
IT MUST HAVE HURT...
ARMIN ...
MY HEAD'S... GOTTEN ALL MESSED UP...
THE FOUNDER'S POWER HAS MADE IT SO THAT THERE'S NO PAST OR FUTURE... IT ALL EXISTS AT ONCE.
SO...
I HAD TO DO IT...

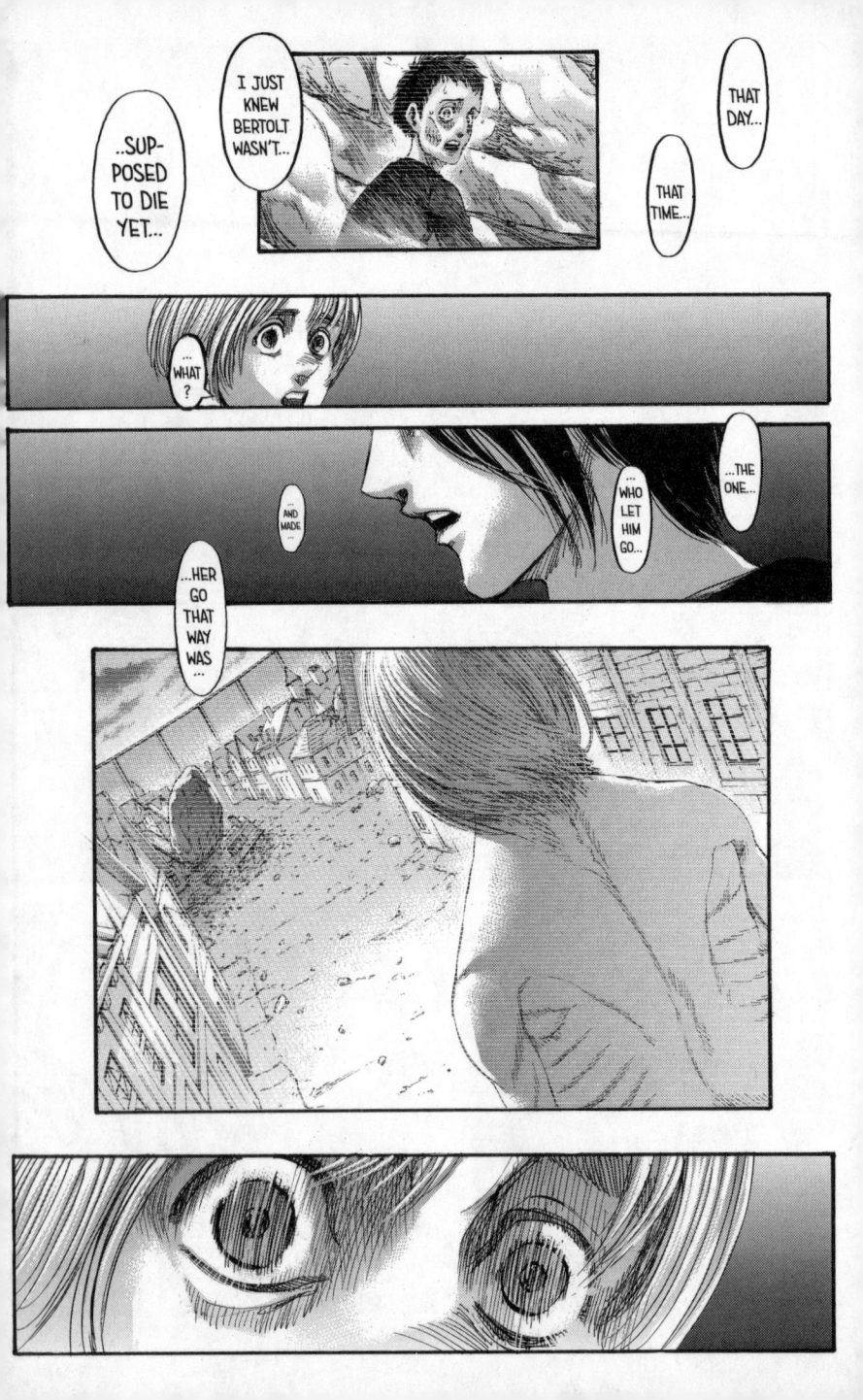
..SUP-POSED TO DIE YET...
I JUST KNEW BERTOLT WASN'T...
THAT TIME...
THAT DAY...
...WHAT?
...THE ONE...
...WHO LET HIM GO...
...AND MADE...
...HER GO THAT WAY WAS...

LET'S GO...
... EREN.
... YEAH.

ABOUT WHAT?
WHAT WERE YOU THINK-ING?
... SO.

ABOUT MIKASA.

WHO KNOWS.
... WELL
JUST LIKE YOU WANTED ...?
DO YOU THINK SHE CAN JUST FORGET ABOUT YOU AND LIVE A HAPPY LIFE WITH SOMEONE ELSE?

I DON'T REMEMBER EVER FORGIVING YOU!
WHAT? WHO KNOWS ?!
... OW!

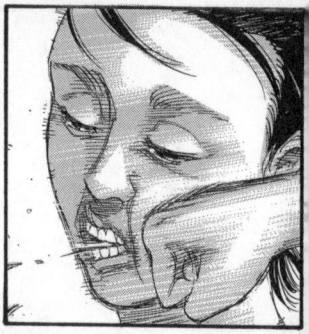

A WOMAN WHO'S ALWAYS VALUED YOU OVER EVERYTHING, EVEN HER OWN LIFE!
WHAT ARE YOU THINKING, DISREGARDING MIKASA'S LOVE FOR YOU LIKE THAT?!
DO YOU REALLY THINK YOU CAN TELL HER TO FORGET ABOUT YOU AND BE DONE WITH IT?!

ON THE OTHER HAND... MAYBE SHE'LL FIND SOME-ONE PERFECT FOR HER IN NO TIME...

SHE SHOULD BE ABLE TO FORGET ABOUT THE HEARTBREAKER SHE LOVED AND BE HAPPY AT THE VERY LEAST!

HM?
..
NO.
NO! I DON'T WANT THAT!
I WANT HER TO THINK ABOUT ME AND NO ONE ELSE FOR THE REST OF HER LIFE!
EVEN AFTER I DIE... I WANT HER TO BE HUNG UP ON ME FOR A WHILE! TEN YEARS, AT LEAST!!
MIKASA FINDING ANOTHER MAN...?!
I...
...PLEASE DON'T REPEAT THAT TO MIKASA...
I WANT HER TO BE HAPPY ...
I REALLY DO. BUT...
...DIDN'T EXPECT SOME-THING THAT PATHETIC ...
AGH... YEAH... DAMMIT...
...
OH.
...
OKAY.

I WANT TO BE WITH MIKASA... WITH EVERYONE.
...I DON'T WANNA DIE.

... NO.
WE CAN FIND ANOTHER WAY...!
EREN ...
DON'T GIVE UP!

...COULD I EVER BE FORGIVEN ...?
HOW ...
BUT ...
I'M SURE NONE OF THEM WANTED TO DIE, EITHER...

EVEN IF I DIDN'T KNOW THAT YOU'D STOP ME IN THE END...
...I THINK I STILL WOULD HAVE FLATTENED THIS WORLD.

... WHY ?

I WANTED... TO LEAVE EVERY SURFACE A BLANK PLAIN...
...AND LEAVE THE LAND COVERED IN CARRION-FATTENED INSECTS A FEW DAYS LATER.
LEVEL ALMOST EVERY FOREST ...

EREN ...
THAT IS YOUR NAME.
... I ...
... DON'T KNOW WHY, BUT...
I WANTED TO DO THAT...
I HAD TO...
EREN ...
YOU ARE FREE...
ARMIN... IT'S TIME.
I'M ERASING ALL YOUR MEMORIES OF THIS PLACE.

NEXT TIME WE MEET, WE'LL BE TRYING TO KILL ONE ANOTHER.
BUT ...
YOU'LL PROBABLY REMEMBER THIS AGAIN ONCE IT'S ALL OVER...

... EREN.
THANK YOU.

I SWEAR I WON'T LET THIS TERRIBLE MISTAKE YOU'RE MAKING BE IN VAIN.

YOU BE-CAME...
...A MASS MURDERER FOR OUR SAKE...

I DON'T KNOW WHAT WILL HAPPEN AFTER I DIE...
BUT I KNOW...
...YOU CAN MAKE IT TO THE OTHER SIDE OF THE WALLS.

HUMANITY WILL BE SAVED...
...BY YOU...

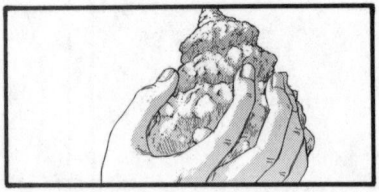

...
ARMIN.

HEALED UP ALREADY ...?
ANNIE ...?
HUH ...?

...NOW I RE-MEM-BER.
THIS IS...
ARMIN.

ARMIN... YOU REMEMBER NOW TOO, DON'T YOU?
WHEN EREN... CAME TO VISIT US.
YEAH.
...I HEARD.
THE RESULT OF YOUR CHOICE...

...WOULD MAKE THE POWER OF THE TITANS...

...VANISH FROM THE FACE OF THIS WORLD.

...NOW I REMEMBER ...
...YOU CONSCIENTIOUS PIECE OF SHIT.
EREN ...
...
YOU REALLY ARE A...
...EREN...
HE SAID EVEN MY MOM WOULD GO BACK..
...TO BEING HUMAN ...
HE SAID ...
... FOR US ...
...TO LIVE LONG ...
WHAT ABOUT YOU ...?
I NEVER ASKED YOU FOR THIS... YOU SUICIDAL BLOCKHEAD...

HUH...
WISH I COULDA TALKED TO HIM...
WEL-COME BACK.
...I'M HOME.
DAD...
GABIIIIIIII
...HEY, GUYS.

YOU SEE THAT?
I GUESS THIS IS IT.
WHAT YOU DEDICATED...
...YOUR HEARTS FOR.

...
SASHA
...

MOM...
I...
I GUESS I'M NOT THE ARMORED TITAN ANYMORE...
...IS THAT SO?
THAT'S... WONDERFUL.
...HUH?
I'M SORRY... FOR EVERYTHING.
REINER...
THIS IS ALL... I EVER NEEDED.

I...
... SHOULD GO.
HUH ?
... WHERE ?
IF I STAYED HERE...
I DOUBT ...
...THEY'D GIVE EREN A PROPER BURIAL.
...
YOU'RE RIGHT.
LET HIM REST SOMEWHERE QUIET...
EREN ...
... ALWAYS LIKED TO NAP THERE.
... YEAH.
I THINK IT'S A GOOD PLACE.

...PLEASE, SECRETARY MULLER.
EREN YEAGER IS DEAD.
THE POWER OF THE TITANS HAS VANISHED...
WE...ARE NOTHING MORE THAN PEOPLE NOW.
CAN YOU PROVE THAT TO ME?
...RIGHT HERE AND NOW?

IF IT'S A BLOOD TEST YOU WANT ...!!
...!!
NOW.
HERE ...
PROVE IT.
PLEASE ...
OR ARE YOU TITANS ...?
ARE YOU HU-MAN...

IF WE DID STILL HAVE THE POWER OF THE TITANS...
...WE'D BE USING IT TO **FIGHT YOU.**
BUT THE FACT THAT WE CONTINUE TO BE POWERLESS EVEN AS YOU POINT YOUR GUNS AT US...
...IS THE GREATEST POSSIBLE PROOF OF OUR HUMANITY.
...
WHO ARE YOU...?

I AM ARMIN ARLERT, AN ELDIAN FROM THE ISLAND OF PARADIS.
AND THE MAN WHO KILLED EREN YEAGER, THE ATTACK TITAN.

SO IT WAS YOU...
YOU WERE THE ONE ALWAYS LOOKING INSIDE MY HEAD...
I'M SURE YOUR LOVE WAS A LONG, LONG NIGHT-MARE.
AND I CAN'T RETURN... THE LIFE THAT WAS STOLEN FROM YOU...
EVEN SO...
THE LIVES YOU GAVE BIRTH TO ARE WHY...
...I'M ALIVE TODAY.

SLEEP WELL.
YMIR.

THREE YEARS HAVE PASSED SINCE THE DAY KNOWN AS THE BATTLE OF HEAVEN AND EARTH.

THOSE WHO SURVIVED AFTER AN UNFATHOMABLE NUMBER OF LIVES WERE TAKEN ARE STILL TORMENTED BY UNHEALING SCARS.
THE NATION OF ELDIA HAS FORMED A SO-CALLED ARMY CONTROLLED BY THE YEAGERISTS, WHO NOW FOCUS THEIR EFFORTS ON BUILDING THEIR MILITARY STRENGTH.
AS THE WORLD SUFFERS THROUGH THIS LOSS, THEIR FEARS HAVE COME TRUE.
...THE ISLAND CRIES OUT AS ONE.
FEARFUL OF RETALIATION FROM WHAT IS LEFT OF HUMANITY ON THE OTHER SIDE OF THE SEA...

IF WE WIN, WE LIVE.
IF WE LOSE, WE DIE.
IF WE DON'T FIGHT, WE CAN'T WIN.
FIGHT.
FIGHT.

THIS FIGHT WILL NOT END UNTIL EITHER ELDIA OR THE WORLD DISAPPEARS.
THAT IS WHAT EREN SAID, AND PERHAPS HE WAS RIGHT AFTER ALL.
EVEN SO, HE CHOSE TO LEAVE THIS WORLD IN OUR HANDS.
AND WE ARE ALIVE, NOW.

IN A WORLD WITHOUT TITANS.
HOW MANY TIMES DO I HAVE TO TELL YOU TO NOT LUST AFTER A MARRIED WOMAN? CREEP.
...I NEVER GET TIRED OF HISTORIA'S BEAUTIFUL HANDWRITING. IT EVEN SMELLS NICE.
DON'T YOU MEAN THE FIELD GUIDE TO HORSES?
...FOR ALL THE GIRLS WHO EVER OPEN A HISTORY TEXTBOOK.
TRYING TO LOOK GOOD FOR SOME-ONE?
YOU SEEM AWFULLY CONCERNED ABOUT HOW YOUR HAIR LOOKS YOUR-SELF, JEAN.
IT'S A DAMN SHAME YOU GOT A NEW LEASE ON LIFE, REINER.

DO YOU REALLY THINK THIS IS GOING TO WORK...?
...ARMIN.
PARADIS IS WITHIN SIGHT NOW.
WE KILLED EREN, A MAN REVERED BY THE PEOPLE OF ELDIA...
AND WE'RE THE ALLIED NATIONS' AMBASSADORS FOR PEACE TALKS...?
WE DESTROYED THE WALLS.
WE BETRAYED THE ISLAND.
I KNOW SHE'LL DEFEND US, TOO.
HER MAJESTY'S FIRST MOVE WAS TO PROTECT JEAN'S RELATIVES AND MY MOM...
BELIEVE IN HISTORIA.
PERSONALLY... I WOULDN'T BE SHOCKED IF THEY SANK OUR SHIP RIGHT HERE.
...THEY'LL HAVE TO WANT TO HEAR...
BUT... WHEN THEY SEE US ALL TOGETHER LIKE THIS...
ANNIE... CONFLICT WILL NEVER VANISH.
US WEAK LITTLE THINGS...

...ABOUT OUR STORY.
WHY THOSE WHO TRIED TO KILL ONE ANOTHER FOR SO LONG...
...HAVE APPEARED ON PARADIS... TO ADVOCATE FOR PEACE.
THEY'LL WANT TO KNOW WHAT WE SAW.

LET'S TELL THEM EVERY-THING...

EREN ...
EVERYONE WILL BE COMING TO VISIT YOU SOON.
ISN'T THAT NICE?

I...
I... MISS YOU SO MUCH...

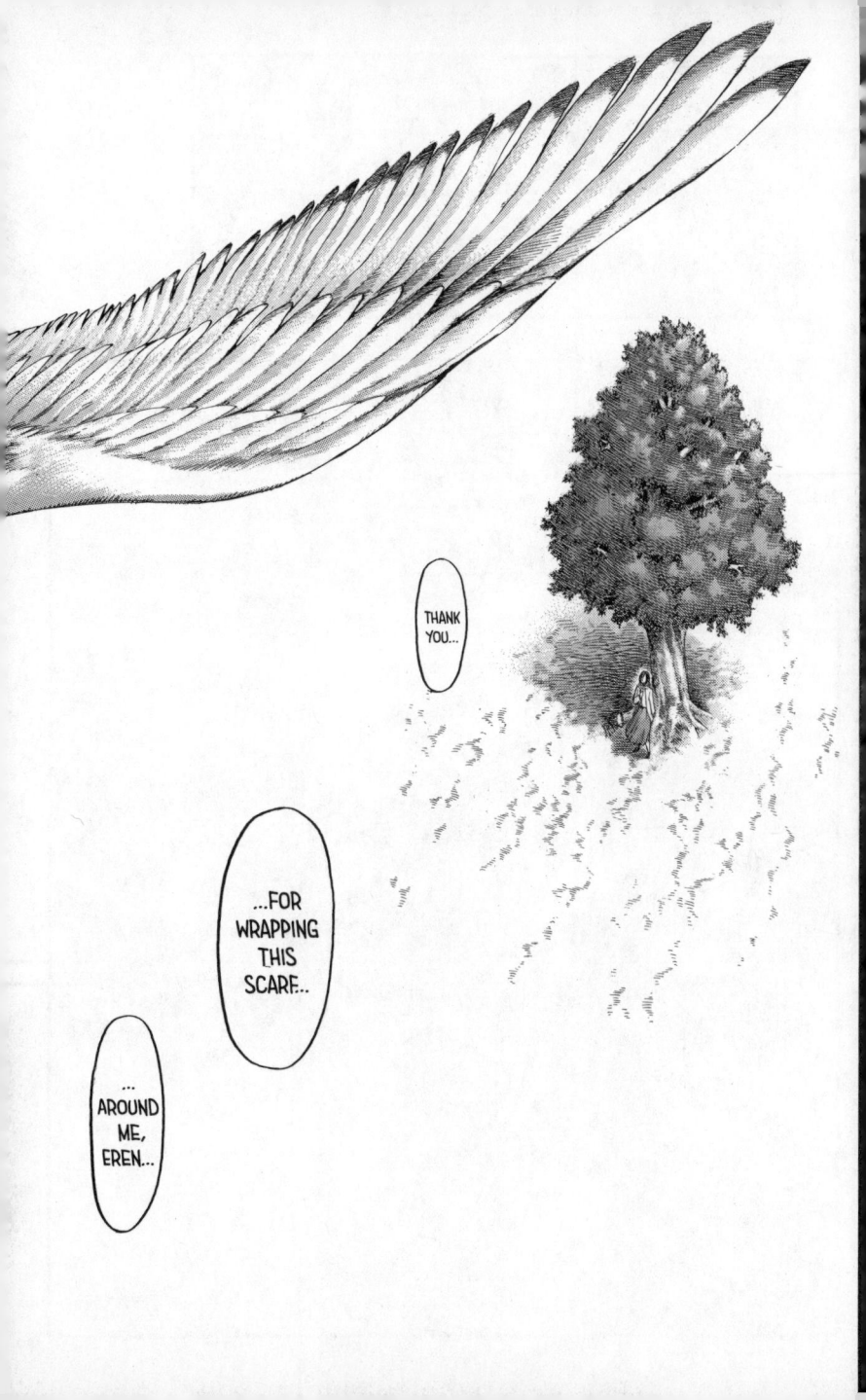
THANK YOU...
...FOR WRAPPING THIS SCARF...
... AROUND ME, EREN...

Attack on Titan
-The End-

ATTACK ON SCHOOL CASTES

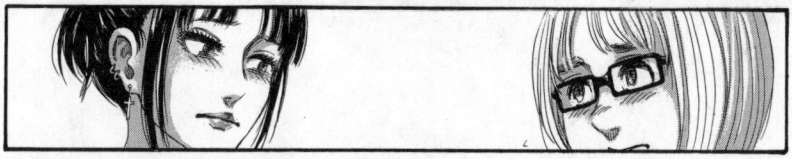

THANK YOU FOR READING!

ATTACK on TITAN

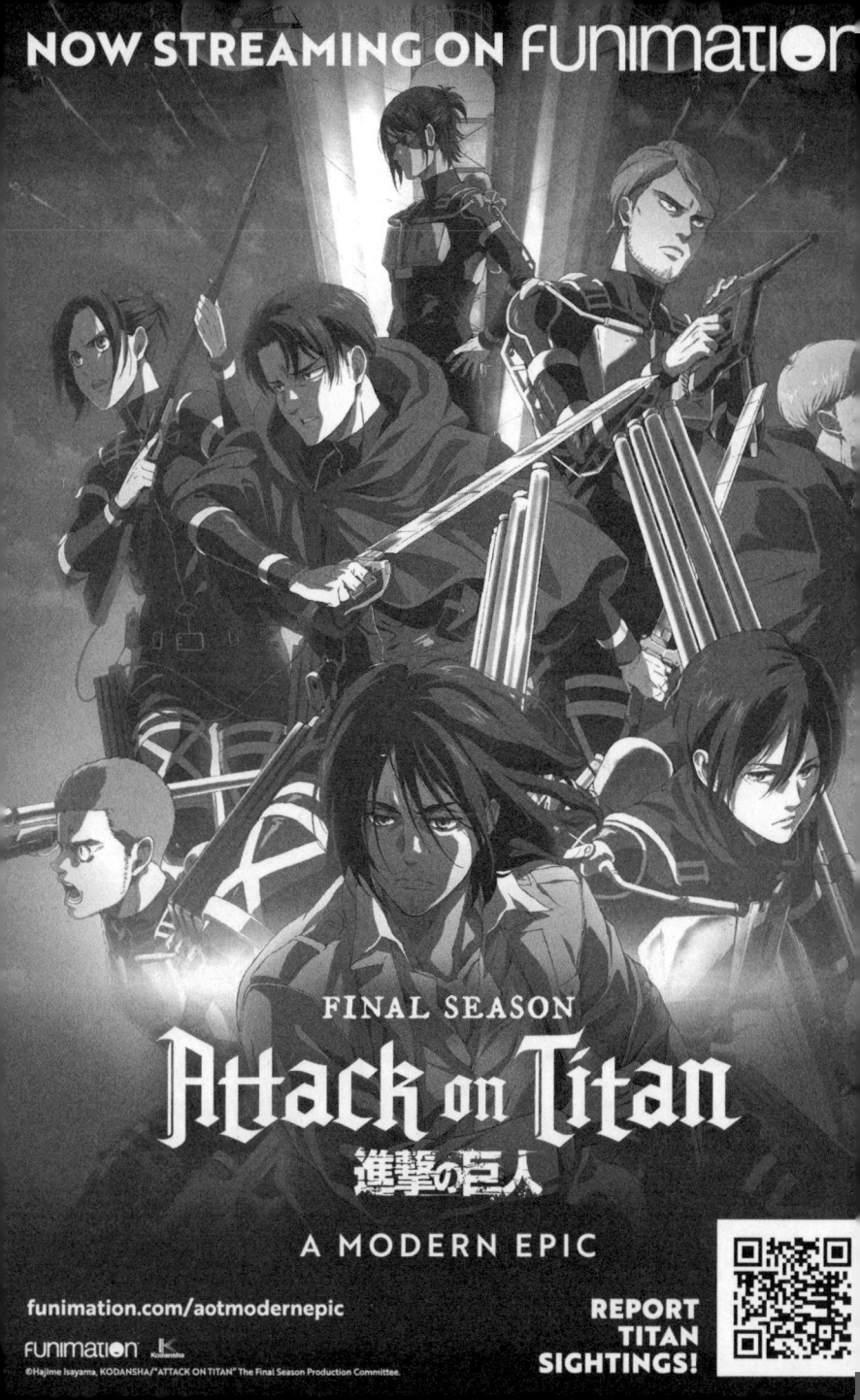
NOW STREAMING ON funimation
FINAL SEASON
Attack on Titan
進撃の巨人
A MODERN EPIC
funimation.com/aotmodernepic
REPORT TITAN SIGHTINGS!
funimation
©Hajime Isayama, KODANSHA/"ATTACK ON TITAN" The Final Season Production Committee.

A SMART, NEW ROMANTIC COMEDY FOR FANS OF *SHORTCAKE CAKE* AND *TERRACE HOUSE*!

Living-Room Matsunaga-san © Keiko Iwashita / Kodansha Ltd.

A romance manga starring high school girl Meeko, who learns to live on her own in a boarding house whose living room is home to the odd (but handsome) Matsunaga-san. She begins to adjust to her new life away from her parents, but Meeko soon learns that no matter how far away from home she is, she's still a young girl at heart — especially when she finds herself falling for Matsunaga-san.

KC KODANSHA COMICS

SKATING THRILLS AND ICY CHILLS WITH THIS NEW TINGLY ROMANCE SERIES!

A rom-com on ice, perfect for fans of *Princess Jellyfish* and *Wotakoi*. Kokoro is the talk of the figure-skating world, winning trophies and hearts. But little do they know... he's actually a huge nerd! From the beloved creator of *You're My Pet* (*Tramps Like Us*).

Chitose is a serious young woman, working for the health magazine *SASSO*. Or at least, she would be, if she wasn't constantly getting distracted by her childhood friend, international figure skating star Kokoro Kijinami! In the public eye and on the ice, Kokoro is a gallant, flawless knight, but behind his glittery costumes and breathtaking spins lies a secret: He's actually a hopelessly romantic otaku, who can only land his quad jumps when Chitose is on hand to recite a spell from his favorite magical girl anime!

PERFECT WORLD

Rie Aruga

A TOUCHING NEW SERIES ABOUT LOVE AND COPING WITH DISABILITY

An office party reunites Tsugumi with her high school crush Itsuki. He's realized his dream of becoming an architect, but along the way, he experienced a spinal injury that put him in a wheelchair. Now Tsugumi's rekindled feelings will butt up against prejudices she never considered — and Itsuki will have to decide if he's ready to let someone into his heart...

"Depicts with great delicacy and courage the difficulties some with disabilities experience getting involved in romantic relationships... Rie Aruga refuses to romanticize, pushing her heroine to face the reality of disability. She invites her readers to the same tasks of empathy, knowledge and recognition."
—Slate.fr

"An important entry [in manga romance]... The emotional core of both plot and characters indicates thoughtfulness... [Aruga's] research is readily apparent in the text and artwork, making this feel like a real story."
—Anime News Network

Perfect World © Rie Aruga/Kodansha Ltd.

THE SWEET SCENT OF LOVE IS IN THE AIR! FOR FANS OF OFFBEAT ROMANCES LIKE *WOTAKOI*

Sweat and Soap © Kintetsu Yamada / Kodansha Ltd.

In an office romance, there's a fine line between sexy and awkward... and that line is where Asako — a woman who sweats copiously — meets Koutarou — a perfume developer who can't get enough of Asako's, er, scent. Don't miss a romcom manga like no other!

KC KODANSHA COMICS

Young characters and steampunk setting, like *Howl's Moving Castle* and *Battle Angel Alita*

KC KODANSHA COMICS

Beyond the Clouds © 2018 Nicke / Ki-oon

A boy with a talent for machines and a mysterious girl whose wings he's fixed will take you beyond the clouds! In the tradition of the high-flying, resonant adventure stories of Studio Ghibli comes a gorgeous tale about the longing of young hearts for adventure and friendship!

The boys are back, in 400-page hardcovers that are as pretty and badass as they are!

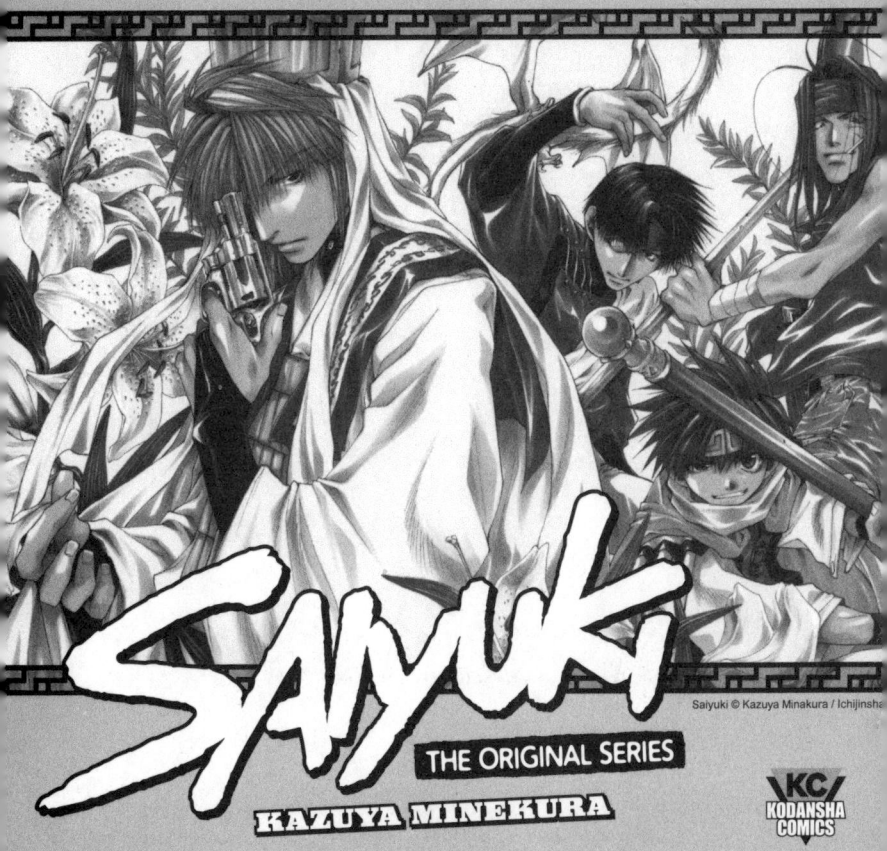

"AN EDGY COMIC LOOK AT AN ANCIENT CHINESE TALE." —YALSA

Genjo Sanzo is a Buddhist priest in the city of Togenkyo, which is being ravaged by yokai spirits that have fallen out of balance with the natural order. His superiors send him on a journey far to the west to discover why this is happening and how to stop it. His companions are three yokai with human souls. But this is no day trip — the four will encounter many discoveries and horrors on the way.

FEATURES NEW TRANSLATION, COLOR PAGES, AND BEAUTIFUL WRAPAROUND COVER ART!

Attack on Titan 34 is a work of fiction. Names, characters, places, and incidents are the products of the author's imagination or are used fictitiously. Any resemblance to actual events, locales, or persons, living or dead, is entirely coincidental.

A Kodansha Comics Trade Paperback Original
Attack on Titan 34 copyright © 2021 Hajime Isayama
English translation copyright © 2021 Hajime Isayama

All rights reserved.

Published in the United States by Kodansha Comics, an imprint of Kodansha USA Publishing, LLC, New York.

Publication rights for this English edition arranged through Kodansha Ltd., Tokyo.

First published in Japan in 2021 by Kodansha Ltd., Tokyo as *Shingeki no kyojin*, volume 34.

Standard Edition
ISBN 978-1-64651-236-2

Barnes & Noble Edition
ISBN 978-1-64651-459-5

BAM Edition
ISBN 978-1-64651-460-1

Kinokuniya Edition
ISBN 978-1-64651-461-8

Original cover design by Takashi Shimoyama/Manami Fukunaga (Red Rooster)

Printed in the United States of America.

www.kodansha.us

9 8 7 6 5 4 3 2 1
Translation: Ko Ransom
Lettering: Dezi Sienty
Editing: Tiff Joshua TJ Ferentini, Ben Applegate
Kodansha Comics edition cover design by Phil Balsman

Publisher: Kiichiro Sugawara

Director of publishing services: Ben Applegate
Associate director of operations: Stephen Pakula
Publishing services managing editors: Alanna Ruse, Madison Salters
Production managers: Emi Lotto, Angela Zurlo